THE
SHOPPING
REVOLUTION

BARBARA E. KAHN

UPDATED AND EXPANDED EDITION

THE SHOPPING REVOLUTION

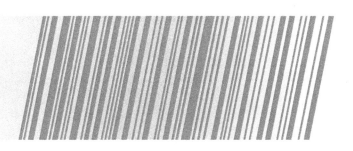

How Retailers Succeed in an Era of Endless Disruption
Accelerated by COVID-19

WHARTON SCHOOL PRESS
Philadelphia

Published by Wharton School Press
The Wharton School
University of Pennsylvania
3620 Locust Walk
2000 Steinberg Hall-Dietrich Hall
Philadelphia, PA 19104
Email: whartonschoolpress@wharton.upenn.edu
Website: http://wsp.wharton.upenn.edu/

Ebook ISBN: 978-1-61363-113-3
Paperback ISBN: 978-1-61363-114-0

I dedicate this book to my husband, Bob Meyer, who patiently and lovingly supported me through the book-writing process, and to my children, Alyssa and Tim, who are always endless sources of inspiration.

Contents

Introduction
How to Compete Successfully in a Retail Apocalypse

C all it an apocalypse. Call it disruption. Call it a revolution. The year 2017, when I was writing the first edition of this book, was a difficult one for the retailing industry in the United States. More than 8,600 stores closed, the highest number in history. It was even worse in 2019, with more than 9,500 stores closing and predictions that 75,000 stores would close across North America by 2026.

But no one was predicting the disaster of the COVID-19 pandemic. From March to June 2020, most nonessential retail was temporarily shuttered, resulting in the closing of 250,000 stores. More than 15,000 stores closed by the end of 2020 in the United States.[1] Although it is difficult to capture the exact number of retail stores closing globally, COVID-19 certainly has had significant adverse effects worldwide.

Can the retailing industry survive? Most definitely. But there is no question that retail as we know it will need to change in dramatic ways.

Retailers are facing a radically transformed marketplace that poses some significant challenges they will need to overcome if they are going to continue to compete—and if they are to avoid the vicious cycle of store closings and bankruptcy.

Although the pandemic was an abrupt disruption to business as usual, mandating a "new normal," many changes were long overdue. Analyses showed that the changes in shopping behavior observed during critical periods of COVID-19 were merely an acceleration of 5 to 10 years of behaviors already in progress.

What forces were responsible for this major transformation in retail? I see seven dominant disruptive trends, which accelerated during COVID-19 but started years before. Beginning with the gorilla in the room—the game-changing dominance of Amazon.

Seven Forces That Are Transforming Retail

There is no singular dynamic at play here. Rather, many different factors have converged to change the face of global retail.

1. The Game-Changing Dominance of Amazon

There is no question Amazon was dominating retail before 2020, but will its dominance be insurmountable after COVID-19? The question is triggering some antitrust investigations. Before COVID-19, Amazon represented nearly 40% of all US online retail sales. In 2020, as a result of the COVID-19 pandemic, including the closing of non-essential physical retailing in the second quarter, net Amazon consumer spending rose between 24% and 33% in the third quarter of 2020 year over year; its advertising business rose 41% year over year; and revenues from Prime memberships were up 29% year over year.[2] A March 2020 survey from RBC Capital Markets found that Amazon was the most popular online grocery destination for new shoppers, with 60% of respondents indicating Amazon was their first choice.[3] This is significant: Although Amazon was the first place to go for online shopping before the pandemic, it was not the first place for online grocery shopping. Amazon's growth, accelerated by its response to COVID-19, is not likely to slow down anytime soon.

But this is just the latest strategic win for Amazon. The company has already completely changed consumers' expectations about shopping. Beginning in 1997, Amazon introduced 1-Click shopping, which eliminated the need for shoppers to reenter payment information every time they made a purchase. This started a long history of innovation in which Amazon systematically removed the pain points in the shopping process. It introduced free shipping, unconventional return policies, dynamic pricing, and personalized recommendations and reviews.

Amazon also offered the "endless aisle," a broad assortment with more than 1 million stock-keeping units (SKUs) available online. It accomplished this by making it easier for small, third-party sellers to sell online through Amazon Marketplace. In 2005, Amazon introduced Amazon Prime, the ultimate loyalty program, which now has tens of millions of members around the world. In 2006, the company launched Amazon Web Services (AWS) to allow small retailers to compete with bigger competitors by providing server capacity. Today, the profitability that comes from AWS, fees from Amazon Marketplace, Amazon Prime, and digital advertising allows Amazon to tighten margins even further in its retail business.

2. Moving from Product-Focused to Customer Retailing in a Customer-Centric Omnichannel World

As consumers first adjusted to the pandemic, they were forced to embrace ecommerce. Thus, people who were already buying online bought more, and people who had never bought online bought for the first time. This shift accelerated the move to ecommerce. In a few short months, ecommerce shopping reached penetration and frequency levels that were not predicted to occur for anywhere from 2 to 10 years, depending on the analysis.

This change in behavior is likely to persist as consumers experience the convenience, safety, and efficiency offered by online channels. Data indicate a 10% higher inclination to purchase online. People will rely more on digital channels for many types of behavior, such as health (telemedicine), fitness (online classes), real estate (virtual tours), and online working arrangements. Trends we had already observed, like streaming entertainment and gaming, will continue to grow. This suggests we will likely see partnerships between retailing and other services that had been difficult to negotiate.

But for consumers, shopping is not really one channel or another; it is an omnichannel experience, which means that consumers expect seamless integration across online, offline, and mobile. For the customer to have a unified experience across all channels and touchpoints, all of the data across platforms have to be connected. And the retailing should be customer-centric, which means a seamless integration across channels should be viewed from the customer perspective—which has been called the third channel and can be facilitated through company apps.

3. Massive Data Collection

With seamless integration across channels, it is possible to record scads of customer data. Mining these data through machine learning allows retailers to personalize and customize shopping experiences.

Personalized offerings include individualized deals at the right time, in the right place. Marketing in general is more tailored, and websites morph as a function of past behavior. Even in-store behavior can be individualized, as consumers learn to use in-store apps to get price and product information.

Better use of data can help retailers adapt to trends more quickly and provide better point-of-sale information. Better data also leads to more accurate forecasting, which can help retailers become leaner and more efficient and make logistics more effective.

To monetize the data in these ways requires both sophisticated data scientists and enough interaction with the customers to be able to draw conclusions. Retailers like Amazon or supermarket retailers can interact with consumers once or twice a week, while others, like department stores, may only be able to capture data from customer interactions two or three times a year. Retailers that do not have high frequency of interaction may have to partner with other entities like Google or Facebook, or even other retailers or brands, to collect information.

New types of retail, like Stitch Fix, offer innovative ways of providing customers with exactly what they want. Stitch Fix is an ecommerce service that delivers a box of fashion, known as a Fix, to a customer using a mix of algorithmic intelligence and human curation. Stitch Fix solicits customers' feedback and measures every aspect of the apparel it sells. A feature called Style Shuffle brings customers back to the app and has them rate items in Stitch Fix's inventory. More than 75% of Stitch Fix's multimillion customers have used the feature, providing more than a billion ratings. From these data, it can offer more personal recommendations, better design products to fit customers' needs, and better optimize its supply chain. Stitch Fix has solved the discovery process for consumers who can be overwhelmed by too many choices. Stitch Fix's algorithms anticipate customers' buying needs and brands' inventory, warehouse, and delivery requirements.

4. New Technologies

In addition to algorithms, important new advances in technology, both in the store and at home, will change shopping experiences.

Retailers have high hopes for virtual reality (VR) and augmented reality (AR). Already it is possible for customers to explore a complete VR environment to determine whether they want to buy a product. For example, Walmart's innovation team designed a buying process for an outdoor tent where the consumer can visualize the tent on a mountaintop in 3D and then get inside it and observe what that feels like.

Progressive retailers have also begun to employ AR, the use of which will likely accelerate owing to the low-touch retailing environments necessitated by COVID-19. Cosmetic retailers can let customers put virtual makeup on their real faces. In home design, customers can put a virtual couch in their real living rooms. Warby Parker uses a combination of facial recognition and AR to allow consumers to try on their glasses; soon, this will extend to eye exams.

Some stores in Beijing and Shanghai are experimenting with contactless shopping, or high-tech fully automated and unstaffed stores that allow people to buy products without checkout lines. US retailers like Amazon and Walmart are also experimenting with this technology.

5. Direct-to-Consumer Retailing

Direct-to-consumer retailing, or vertical integration, incorporates the retail value chain so that the brand does the manufacturing, branding, and distribution. Products go directly from the factory to the consumer through the brand's website, retail store, or showroom, eliminating the need for partners and additional margins. This allows companies to sell higher-quality products at lower prices.

Luxury brands are also going direct—not necessarily to lower prices, but to increase service, customization, and control of the brand heritage.

Many new "digitally native vertical brands" feature price transparency as part of their customer value. Vertical integration has allowed for shorter delivery times, better return policies, and full access to customer information and inventory management.

Direct-to-consumer strategies also protect some retailers and brands from Amazon's ruthless pricing strategies. For example, Nike has stopped selling on Amazon's platform and has accelerated plans to retail to its customers directly, providing the company with better control of quality and customer experience.

6. Over-Storing of America

With or without the pandemic, there was bound to be a shakeout in physical retailing, because America was "over-stored." There was too much supply.

Between 1970 and 2013, the number of malls in the United States grew more than twice as fast as the population. The United States had 5 times more shopping spaces per capita than the United Kingdom and 10 times more than Germany.

The industry had been building new stores faster than consumers could spend in them. There are several reasons for the missed forecasts. In some cases, developers built more stores in areas where the population was decreasing, like in Cleveland. In other areas, like Phoenix and Atlanta, stores were built in anticipation of population increases that didn't occur because of the housing bubble. The Great Recession didn't help, because people started spending less.

Certainly, one lasting effect of the COVID-19 pandemic will be the massive closing of stores, as a result of bankruptcies, the economic crisis, and changing shopping behavior. We are likely to see the continuation and proliferation of "buy online, pick up in the store" (BOPIS) and curbside pickup. Some retail space is also being converted to warehouse and fulfillment centers to help facilitate home delivery.

7. A New Generation of Customers: Generation Z

The media have been replete with discussion of the power of millennials. Accenture estimates their spending power will be $1.4 trillion by 2020, representing 30% of all sales.[4] But there is a new generation in town. Generation Z, or "Gen Z"—those born starting in the mid-1990s and just entering college now—was projected to make up 40% of the consumer base by 2020; they influence family spending as well. One estimate puts their buying power at $44 billion.

One big difference between millennials and Gen Z is that millennials experienced the Great Recession, while Gen Z grew up in flusher times—amid the pandemic, it remains to be seen what the long-term effect on shopping behavior will be. Pre-COVID-19, though, Gen Z shoppers had been somewhat less price conscious than millennials. They are also more attuned to sustainability issues.

Gen Z is not as brand loyal as past generations, because they are used to seeing new digital brands spring up virtually overnight. They are comfortable giving up their personal data when appropriate, but they are also sophisticated enough to demand that their data be protected.

Like millennials, Gen Z consumers are digitally native and comfortable with online shopping. These new shoppers are not shunning physical stores, but they have different expectations. They expect and embrace technology in stores; they are comfortable with interactive shopping screens, self-checkout, and virtual try-on. While they expect stores to offer fun, experiential, interactive shopping experiences, they also expect convenience. And they have little tolerance: Stores that don't deliver fall out of favor.

Gen Z consumers do not want to own "things" to the same degree as their parents. They prefer experiences. Partly, this is because they get currency from sharing photos on social media. They are more likely to rent or share products. As they embrace these trends, older Americans follow.

Gen Z consumers are also comfortable omnichannel shoppers and are quite used to using their phones in tandem with their in-store shopping. They value consumer reviews. They are sophisticated with price comparisons; they have more access to price data and use price calculators. But that doesn't mean they don't appreciate luxury. As with other generations, there is great heterogeneity in price sensitivity.

They are also comfortable searching for information for themselves before they make purchases, so they are more demanding, and they expect more from in-store sales associates. Social media is part of their everyday lives. They share photographs of experiences and products with their networks.

How Can Retailers Compete in This Marketplace?

One of the keys to Amazon's success in disrupting retail in the mid-1990s is a fierce understanding of what customers want. Winning retailers have to be completely customer-centric. This means they need to be mindful not only of what products customers want but also of the importance of convenience—removing the pain of shopping.

In addition, given the competition in the marketplace today, it is important to not only fill customers' needs, but to do so in a way that is even better than the competition. This requires gathering massive amounts of customer data, as well as pinpointing competitive actions and anticipating future innovation and response. Finally, it is essential to keep pace with ever-changing technologies.

As scary as the Amazon threat appears, a number of retailers are doing quite well in this new world. That is the ultimate purpose of *The Shopping Revolution*—to explain how they are doing it.

Why I Wrote This Book

As professor of marketing at the Wharton School of the University of Pennsylvania, I have had the unique opportunity to study the changing retail landscape for many years. From January 2011 through July 2017, I directed the Jay H. Baker Retailing Center at the Wharton School.

Throughout those years, and since, I have had extensive conversations with CEOs and C-suite executives of the largest retailers in the country, including Macy's, Saks, Lord & Taylor, Nordstrom, Ralph Lauren, Tory Burch, Costco, Walmart/Jet.com, Victoria's Secret, Barneys, LVMH, Estée Lauder, Stuart Weitzman, Nike, BJ's, Foot Locker, Sephora, Michael Kors, Coach, PVH, Alice and Olivia, Burlington, Perry Ellis, Vince, Ascena, Spirit, Walgreens/Duane Reade, Haddad Brands, Delta Galil, Modell's, and Williams-Sonoma, among many others. I have also had the opportunity to talk with some of the newer startups like Warby Parker, Bonobos, Birchbox, Harry's, Allbirds, Glossier, Story, Tommy John, Eataly, Rebecca Minkoff, Everlane, Stitch Fix, and many others. In China, I met with representatives from JD.com, Alibaba, PDD, Little Red Book, Farfetch, VIP.com, TikTok, and Fresh.

My deep immersion in retail research led me to understand what it takes for companies to compete. I have distilled those insights into a strategic framework that explains both how successful companies are surviving and thriving in today's retail environment and where opportunities exist for retailers that need a more competitive strategy, as well as startups looking for a way in.

When the first edition of this book was published in 2018, it received a very positive reception. Featured in the *New York Times*,

Bloomberg, and *Vox, The Shopping Revolution* was called a "brilliant analysis of the disruptive effect that Amazon is having on the retail industry and how stores can fight back in order to survive," according to *Forbes*'s Walter Loeb. I received many invitations to speak on the topic, and the book was translated and published in simplified and complex Chinese, Vietnamese, and Portuguese. This updated and expanded version reflects the changes that have occurred in the retailing industry, even in the short time since it was first published, including responses demanded by reactions to COVID-19. Although the pandemic caused some retailers to go bankrupt, it created opportunities for others, and the innovative retailers that were able to pivot quickly gained significant advantages. In addition to the updates, I have added a new chapter that outlines some of the retailing innovations happening in China. Chinese retailing can serve as a blueprint for possible future retailing scenarios here in the United States.

In chapter 1, I introduce the Kahn Retailing Success Matrix, which is built on two simple marketing principles:

1. Customers want to buy something they want (product benefits) from someone they trust (customer experience).
2. To win customers, retailers must offer products and experiences that are better than the competition's.

In the chapters that follow, I break down the strategies of dozens of winning companies using this matrix. In chapter 2, you'll read about how Amazon's laser focus on customer convenience has been a winning strategy. In chapter 3, I explore how Walmart and other retailers leverage low prices to be leaders. In chapter 4, I focus on how direct-to-consumer brands are winning, from Warby Parker, Bonobos, and Casper to Trader Joe's and Zara. In chapter 5, you'll learn about the retail strategies for luxury, where low prices and accessibility are undesirable. In chapter 6, we'll look at how to compete on customer experience. Eataly, the luxury Italian gourmet food, restaurant, and cooking-school emporium, the treasure hunt experiences offered by Costco and T.J.Maxx, and the exciting ever-changing beauty landscape in Sephora all demonstrate the lure of emotional and sensory engagement. Finally, in chapter 7, brand new to this edition, I look at how retailing is developing in China and explore ways we can learn from their "new retail."

As Al Sambar, a retail expert at Kurt Salmon, says, "If you understand your customer enough to be the exclusive provider they trust to bring them a product or service they desire, then you have nothing to worry about from Amazon. But most brands should assume their consumers interact with Amazon 10 to 50 times more frequently than they do in their current distribution channels. Trust follows frequency. Amazon is winning frequency in a landslide. So even the best brands must be wary."[5]

Competing in this ever-changing marketplace isn't easy, but it can be done if you're committed to starting the journey now.

Chapter 1

Gain a Competitive Edge
The Kahn Retailing Success Matrix

In This Chapter
- The Kahn Retailing Success Matrix
- Four Leadership Strategies That Offer Superior Value

How did Amazon become the retailer of choice for a large portion of the US population? How did Walmart beat out other grocers in the late 1990s to become the leader in food retailing? How did Warby Parker make a dent in the once-untouchable Luxottica's lucrative eyewear business? How did Sephora draw customers away from once-dominant department stores to become the go-to retailer for beauty products?

The answer is that each of these retailers raised customers' expectations in at least one key dimension of value: Walmart focused on low cost. Amazon looked to convenience. Warby Parker offered hip, branded eyewear to millennials. And Sephora strived to provide a superior in-store customer experience. Each, then, became the market leader to targeted segments of customers and has enjoyed enormous success.

But in today's competitive world of retailing, keeping a leadership position based on only one aspect of customer value—one area of excellence—is not sufficient. That's why each of these companies has also leveraged its inherent advantage in one dimension and offered excellence on a *second* dimension.

Today, Amazon not only offers convenience in shopping but also guarantees very low prices. Building on its operational excellence and guaranteed lowest price strategy, Walmart purchased Jet.com to build up Walmart.com and provide a better omnichannel experience. Warby Parker eliminated the middleman to offer eyeglasses directly to the end user, providing significant cost savings. Sephora built a huge loyalty program that combines in-store and online shopping behavior to provide a personalized, convenient experience for each of its customers.

These retailers offer individual examples of successful strategies. To generalize these successful approaches so any retailer can map out a strategic plan, I built a framework flexible enough to use across different retailing verticals and different customer segments. Because of the framework's origins on basic assumptions, the strategic implications generalize beyond retailing to other industries.

Mapping Successful Retail Strategies: The Kahn Retailing Success Matrix

Most classic frameworks of retail strategy are missing a critical dimension: the customer perspective. It is a significant and startling omission.

After all, when customers go shopping, they want to buy something they *value* (product benefits) from someone they *trust* (customer experience). More than ever, this idea of trust is critical. Customers demand that retailers and brands offer value to society and that their business practices not be exploitative or deceptive. Providing genuine value will result in long-term customer loyalty.

Customers have lots of choices, and they gravitate to the retailers that offer them the best value on the dimensions they care about. In other words, retailers have to provide some kind of *superior competitive advantage* beyond what is being offered by the competition. This superior value can be delivered either by providing a more trustworthy or pleasurable experience or by removing pain and inconvenience from the retail experience.

Figure 1.1. The Kahn Retailing Success Matrix

	Product Benefits	Customer Experience	
Superior Competitive Advantage	**Product Brand** Branded performance superiority WARBY PARKER LV NIKE	**Experiential** Enhanced customer experience EATALY SEPHORA	*Increase Trust/ Pleasure*
	Low Price Operational excellence, lowest costs, efficiencies Walmart COSTCO WHOLESALE TJ·maxx Burlington	**Frictionless** Comprehensive customer understanding and total convenience amazon	*Eliminate Pain Points*

Retail Proposition

These two ideas result in a simple 2×2 matrix that is surprisingly effective at categorizing the most successful retailing strategies today. The framework is very flexible and is therefore relevant across different verticals. Plotting strategy on this framework also provides a mechanism to measure progress at delivering this value relative to customers' expectations and competitors' actions (see figure 1.1).

The "Retail Proposition," the horizontal axis of this 2×2 matrix, represents the first principle: Customers want to buy something they want (product benefits) from someone they trust (customer experience). "Superior Competitive Advantage," the vertical axis, represents the second principle: In order to win customers, retailers must offer products and experiences that are better than the competition's.

This matrix spells out four basic strategies. The first two strategies, illustrated on the top row, differentiate themselves by providing a more trustworthy relationship with the consumer and by providing more pleasure and more benefits; the second two strategies, illustrated on the bottom row, differentiate by eliminating pain points.

1. Lead on Brand: Offer Branded Product Superiority

Retailers in the Product Brand quadrant offer branded products that provide more differentiation, more value, more pleasure, and ultimately more trust with a particular customer segment, as compared with other products on the market. Here I am specifically referring to the value that comes from branded product. It is the product's brand equity that brings the customer into the store.

There are several ways retailers can leverage the value offered through products that have strong brand equity. First, there are multibrand retailers that carry multiple lines of strong branded products that "pull" the customer into the store. Good examples include Nordstrom, Best Buy, or Kroger. The retailer's own brand name may also be a draw, but here the differentiated focus is on the well-known and well-respected branded products. These retailers may also offer private-label or store brands, but these brands typically differentiate by offering some kind of price advantage—rather than the quality and superiority offered by the more powerful brands.

Other retailers in this quadrant include high-quality brands that are sold directly to the end user. These are known as vertical brands, and the product brand name is the same as the retailer's brand name. Examples include luxury brands like Louis Vuitton or Hermès, specialty retailers such as Lululemon or Zara, or the newer digitally native vertical brands such as Warby Parker or Glossier.

In all of these cases, these brands have developed deep emotional connections with consumers and a strong narrative; their customers frequently become brand advocates. In the luxury markets, these brands have heritage, exclusivity, and prestige. For the nonluxury brands, they have strong identity and values that resonate with their devotees. These brands offer a "point of view"—and a brand culture that consumers want to be associated with.

In addition to strongly branded products, retailers that excel in this strategy are typically very good merchants. Retailing analyst and journalist Walter Loeb describes merchandising as the "instinctual ability to choose the right items to round out merchandise presentations."

He continues: "The best merchants intuitively know how to select products with care and make sure that their newest assortments are fashion-right, fresh, attractive and in sync with other merchandise their buyers had bought before."[6]

Retailers in this quadrant also excel in design and style. The challenge is to be able to accurately predict the "next" trend. The product assortments have to be easy to process and aligned with the brand values; this usually involves curation (especially in physical stores) or the right filtering and categorization structure if the assortments are online, as well as catering to the "long tail." Finally, leaders in this quadrant may also compete on state-of-the-art technology. All in all, the leaders here succeed in developing an innovative culture where new ideas are embraced and commercialized quickly.

2. Lead on Experiential: Offer Enhanced Customer Experience

Physical retailers competing in the Experiential quadrant are always challenged to bring customers through the door. Amid the COVID-19 pandemic, retailers have had an even higher hurdle to entice customers into their stores. First and foremost, the customer has to feel safe in the physical environment. Second, the physical experience has to offer something more than an online alternative. People may choose to go to physical stores because of immediacy, because they want to touch and feel the product, or because they want the security of the social interaction. But to be a real leader in this quadrant, the retailer has to create an experience that provides the customer with more pleasure, more excitement, and more fun than other retailers.

Post-pandemic retailers have had to move to a low-touch environment for safety reasons, but they still want to offer the benefits the high-touch milieu used to provide. This has necessitated changes for retailers like Eataly, Whole Foods, Trader Joe's, Lululemon, and Sephora, which have had to adapt but still want to bring consumers joy. Sampling foods or trying on makeup or new clothes is trickier amid the pandemic, but sophisticated retailers have figured out ways to continue to make the in-store environment more experiential. New techniques involve leveraging technologies like AR or developing clever new packaging alternatives or dressing-room options to offer sanitary solutions. Figuring out ways to add in the social element but still provide the necessary social distancing has also been part of the new equation.

Even traditional retailers can add experiential components to routine shopping tasks. Duane Reade has divided its stores into health, beauty, and food centers—each of which offers high-touch experiences such as clinical access, hair and nail services, and in-store food services. Costco makes the shopping experience fun by training customers to understand that they can never know for sure which brands will be carried at any particular time. This promotes excitement and discovery in-store. T.J.Maxx and Burlington also promote this kind of treasure hunt experience, which encourages customers to come back to the store frequently to see what unexpected brands and styles are available.

Other experiential retailers offer education. For example, Eataly and H-E-B offer cooking and wine classes as well as catering services. Sephora and Ulta allow customers to experiment and learn about their products in-store. Showroom models, like those of Warby Parker and Bonobos, allow customers to interact with knowledgeable sales associates, then purchase the products they want online.

Another avenue that retailers have used to supplement the in-store customer experience involves becoming part of the local community. Some of the more successful retailers have become community centers, such as the Apple store. Other retailers (before COVID-19) have hosted events such as book readings, celebrity talks, and community get-togethers. Lifestyle brands, like Nike or Lululemon, often offer aerobic or yoga classes, rock-climbing walls, or basketball courts. Pop-up stores within stores can create excitement, "newness," and showcase innovation.

Brands can also add experiential components through the digital shopping interface. Some of the most creative experiential strategies are being debuted in China with shoppertainment and livestreaming (see chapter 7). Stitch Fix provides a particularly innovative customer experience that is redefining shopping. Stitch Fix relies on the customer's inputted preferences as well as sophisticated algorithms based on artificial intelligence (AI), which are then edited by expert stylists, to choose personally curated items for each customer. There is a style fee every time customers order a box, or a Fix, which contains several items from which customers can choose what they like while sending back the rest.

3. Lead on Low Price: Offer Operational Excellence, Lowest-Cost Efficiencies

Retailers in the Low Price quadrant provide reliable products or services at the lowest prices, and therefore offer customers the most savings. Retailers that can consistently offer the lowest prices have developed operating models that can efficiently manage inventory, keep overhead costs down, eliminate unnecessary intermediary steps, and reduce transaction costs at every step. Good examples include Walmart, Costco, T.J.Maxx, and Burlington.

Retailers that deliver operational excellence strategies, as defined originally by Michael Treacy and Fred Wiersema in *The Discipline of Market Leaders* (1995), are companies that look for creative ways to minimize overhead costs and eliminate unnecessary transaction costs. They also offer reliability and efficiency, excellent customer service, and strong customer-focused policies for returns. These retailers build their entire business models around these goals.

The leaders in this category often identify a creative means for achieving cost advantages over and above the competition. In pursuing a low-price strategy, Warby Parker founders and co-CEOs Neil

Blumenthal and Dave Gilboa recognized that if they sold eyeglasses directly to the end users online (when 98% of the purchases were historically made in physical stores), they could reduce margins significantly.

In the 1960s, Sam Walton, who founded Walmart, recognized that the "high-low" pricing strategies that were being used by most grocers at the time resulted in uneven demand and high costs in managing inventory and distribution. To correct these inefficiencies, he implemented an "everyday low pricing" (EDLP) strategy that allowed Walmart to significantly reduce costs by reducing the costly peaks and valleys in demand. He supplemented these cost savings by revolutionizing the way retail companies manage their supply chains. Walmart practiced unprecedented coordination with its suppliers, sharing real-time sales data with the manufacturers that stock its shelves.

4. Lead on Frictionless: Offer Comprehensive Customer Understanding and Total Convenience

Retailers in the Frictionless quadrant prioritize providing a frictionless customer experience that eliminates all pain points and offers the customer the easiest and most convenient way to shop. The key deliverable here is a simple, seamless integration of the shopping experience across all touchpoints. This requires the capture and analysis of all available customer data. Constantly analyzing the data allows for customization and personalization. The best example here is Amazon—first through its online platform, subsequently via its integration with physical-store pickups, lockers, and its own stores, and eventually through data collected in the connected home. Amazon also competes effectively in this quadrant by offering one place to shop for all needs. Amazon has been called the "everything store." This ability to buy whatever you want whenever you want makes shopping convenient and easier. This also allows Amazon to have more interactions with consumers, which provides more data.

To succeed here, retailers must identify the current pain points in the shopping experience. For example, in a survey of more than 2,000 consumers conducted in February 2017 by the Adyen payment platform, the most common consumer complaint in physical stores—one mentioned by more than 75% of respondents—was waiting in line.[7] The second most common focused on pushy salespeople, with the third being pressure to make a purchase in the store. These pain points became even more important in the COVID-19 era.

Other surveys have delivered similar results, with more respondents than ever indicating they would rather interact with their mobile phone when shopping in-store than actually talk to a salesperson. However, these trends should not be read as an indication that there is no value to the physical location; in contrast to the complaints, 60% of the respondents indicated they enjoyed the ability to touch and try on products in stores, as well as the instant gratification of walking away with a purchase.

Taken together, these data suggest a key deliverable for retailers operating in this quadrant has to be a painless, seamless integration of the shopping experience across all consumer touchpoints.

The challenge here is what Kurt Salmon once called the "digital experience paradox." In this world of the Internet of Things, the digital touchpoints are increasing—but notably, these touchpoints are controlled by the consumer, not the retailer. So, retailers must leverage the data, gain consumers' total trust, and proactively meet their needs to keep them loyal.

Loyalty metrics such as customer acquisition and retention costs, lifetime value of the customer, and churn rates help retailers identify their most profitable customers and make sure their needs are being met. Retailers that are succeeding in this quadrant are constantly increasing the number of touchpoints they have with their customers and using machine learning, AI chat bots, and other strategies to systematize the customer experience and proactively anticipate customers' future needs and desires.

Plotting Retailers' Competitive Positions
on the Kahn Retailing Success Matrix

The Kahn Retailing Success Matrix provides a way to categorize different winning strategies, but it doesn't on its own provide strategic guidance. To add that dimension, it is useful to think of the center point of the grid as the origin or (0,0) point of each of the four separate axes. On each of these axes, we can plot customers' perceptions for any retailer at delivering value given that specific strategy. The farther out (toward the four corners) retailers are on each of the axes, the better their performance on that dimension; the closer they are to the (0,0) point, the less effective they are at delivering the value. For example, if a retailer's performance on the experiential store-experience axis is plotted near the origin, consumers view that experience as subpar. If the store experience scores high, like that of Sephora, that rating would be plotted as farther away from the origin.

However, it is difficult for consumers to evaluate retailers in the abstract. It is much easier for them to determine whether a retailer is above or below their expectations for value for each dimension. Therefore, before we plot a retailer's score on each dimension, we need to anticipate what the consumers' threshold expectations are: What is the fair value or bare minimum that a retailer has to deliver to be considered acceptable by the consumer on each of the four axes? Anything that falls below that threshold would be considered inferior performance—and retailers that deliver inferior performance cannot survive in a competitive marketplace. For example, RadioShack stores were below customer threshold expectations on several of the dimensions, and as a result, the retailer went out of business.

In figure 1.2, these fair-value expectations are plotted as hash marks on each axis. The customers' expectations are all drawn equidistant from the origin, but this does not have to be the case. The farther out the customers' threshold expectations are from the origin, the higher the expectations are on that dimension, representing

Figure 1.2. The Kahn Retailing Success Matrix: Plotting a Competitive Position

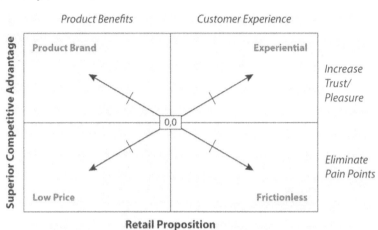

a more competitively difficult market in which to compete and win. To measure these fair-value thresholds, dedicated market research should be conducted to see what consumers are expecting.

After the customer expectations are plotted, the firm's own position can be plotted on these axes, relative to the fair-value or threshold expectations. Is the firm delivering below or above customers' expectations on each of these dimensions?

Ever-Changing Customer Expectations

To survive, retailers must aspire to be at least at fair value in all of the quadrants. But to be a market leader, retailers must provide *superior* value—and literally be the best, if possible—in at least one quadrant. In addition, in competitive markets, it is necessary to be tops in two of the quadrants.

If each of the retailing titans strives for leadership positions and offers superior value above and beyond customers' threshold expectations on any specific dimension, this will inevitably shape what customers come to expect and, in time, demand. As each retailer strives to win and offers something of ever-greater value to the customer, this new advantage becomes the new standard for fair value—and the new expected requirement to compete effectively.

For example, when a particular retailer makes the commitment to offer two-day delivery—or even same-day delivery—the expectations ratchet up as to what is fair value in delivery timing. As the industry becomes more competitive, customers' expectations move farther and farther out to the corners, and it becomes more difficult to compete. Amazon has raised customers' expectations as to what should be expected from a frictionless shopping experience. Sephora has proved that customers want to interact and sample its beauty products themselves and are no longer content to wait for a sales associate to pull the product out from behind the counter.

To be competitive, retailers have to constantly keep track of customer expectations and make sure they are at least delivering value up to what is needed. This is forever challenging, because competitors that are actively trying to take over as market leader cause these expectations to constantly increase.

Winning Leadership Strategies

The final step is to plot out a winning strategy. In the very competitive world of retail, a winning strategy requires leadership in one quadrant that is then leveraged to provide leadership in a second quadrant. This requires maniacal focus on strengths and on developing business models that pave the way to dominance.

Historically, strategic frameworks have suggested that market leaders should be the best at *one* thing and then good enough at everything else to win customers over. The argument was that if firms tried to be good at everything, they would not succeed, and would end up being "not good enough" at anything or "stuck in the middle," whereas those firms that focused on one strategy would end up with a leadership position.

However, given intense competition and ruthless disruption of the retailing industry, I argue that being the best at one value discipline is now insufficient. Retailers must build on their initial strengths to win on at least one other dimension—while also not ignoring the rest.

In the nonleadership quadrants, companies must deliver only up to customers' fair-value expectations. In other words, in these other dimensions, "good enough" will often suffice. Indeed, retailers should actually be wary of trying to be more than "good enough" on the nondominant quadrants, because any additional efforts could strain resources that would be better directed toward leadership strengths.

Since all customers are different and have different value priorities, some will be attracted to different retailers depending on the customer's unique needs. The choice of which strategy to pursue should depend on the firm's historical strengths, where it believes it can offer a significant differential competitive value over and above what the competition can deliver, as well as the various weights different customer segments apply to each of the dimensions. Notably, some customer segments may be more lucrative than others. Leadership depends on offering superior value in two quadrants and meeting fair value in the other two. But offering fair value in the nondominant quadrants can be challenging because customers' expectations are constantly increasing as they learn what retailing leaders are willing to offer.

The importance of the relative dimensions will vary by retailing vertical and by customer segment. Further, movements along the axes may have different cost profiles. Plotting one's positions and your competitors' positions over time, as well as recording changing customer expectations, will provide a dynamic map for keeping track of market performance.

Going back to the examples at the start of this chapter and plotting those retailing leaders' strategies on the grid provides proof that companies must become leaders by winning in two quadrants. These Two-Quadrant Winning Strategies are illustrated in figure 1.3. Amazon and Walmart are trying to be leaders by removing pain points from both the product and the customer experience; however, they start from different strengths. Warby Parker leverages its strong

Figure 1.3. Two-Quadrant Winning Strategies

Amazon

Walmart

Warby Parker, Zara

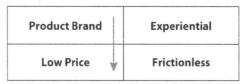

T.J.Maxx, Costco, Luxury, Sephora

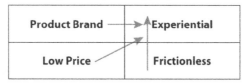

brand name to gain customers but would probably not be successful if it did not also offer a lower-price advantage. That is similarly the case with Zara. Sephora builds on its superior customer loyalty program to offer unparalleled customer experiences in its stores. Luxury brands have learned that offering top branded products is not sufficient; they also must follow through with luxurious customer experiences. Costco and T.J.Maxx do not merely rely on low price but also offer a treasure hunt experience to lure customers into their stores.

Conclusion

The retailing industry is competitive, and new technologies are disrupting old models at a frantic pace. Successful retailers must constantly monitor their competitors and track changing consumer demands and expectations. The Kahn Retailing Success Matrix suggests the way for retailers to win in such a challenging marketplace is to be the leader in one of the four quadrants and to build on this strength to catch up to the leaders in a second quadrant. This is illustrated in the "arrow" strategy, depicted in figure 1.3.

The model does not suggest that the other two quadrants should be ignored, but it is impossible to be the best at everything. It is only necessary to compete at fair value in these two quadrants, rather than looking for a leadership position.

A company's choice in strategy will depend on that retailer's inherent strengths and the culture of the organization, and ultimately will set priorities for future allocation of resources. Customers are attracted to different retailers depending on their own needs, so the choice of strategy will inevitably attract specific customer segments—and, by extension, inevitably turn away others.

The Kahn Retailing Success Matrix provides a graphing mechanism that allows changes in marketplace dynamics to be recorded over time. In the chapters that follow, I will use this framework to plot various successful retailers' strategies. I won't be using actual data to plot these strategies, but rather will use the tool as a way to communicate the strategic choices simply and clearly.

Chapter 2

Amazon the Disruptor
Laser Focus on the Customer and Reducing Friction in the Shopping Experience

In This Chapter: Kahn Retailing Success Strategy
- Key Leadership Strength: Frictionless, Pain-Free, Convenient Customer Experience
- Secondary Leadership Strength: Low-Price Leader
- Fair Value in Branded Product and Experiential Quadrants

If Walmart was the retailing juggernaut of the 1990s, there is no question that Amazon holds that title today. And the difference in Amazon's strategy compared with its competition is even more extreme than the era in which Walmart essentially put America's mom-and-pop retailers out of business. It is not an exaggeration to say that Amazon has fundamentally changed the shopping experience.

The numbers verify these claims. Amazon's annual revenues in 2019 were more than $280.5 billion, with a net income of $11.59 billion. It is the number one internet retailer in the United States, with 37.7% market share in 2019, according to eMarketer.[8] Amazon's share of the total US retail market is 4%. Although the retailer with the highest overall retail sales, both online and offline, is still Walmart (as a comparison, Walmart's share of US retailing spend is 8.9%), Amazon carries 30 times the SKUs of Walmart and is the top online seller in Europe and Japan. Amazon is also strong in India, which it entered in 2013 (by contrast, the company is still lagging in China because of fierce competition from Alibaba and JD.com).

Amazon's stated mission is to be the earth's most customer-centric company—offering the best price, the largest selection, and the fastest delivery. To achieve this goal, Amazon continually reinvests profits in R&D and has repeatedly turned out state-of-the-art innovations that attract more and more customers to its platform.

In 2020, Amazon grew even stronger when other retailers were faltering due to the effects of COVID-19. In the early stages of the pandemic, the reliance on Amazon as one of the few retailers that could continue operations exerted a huge strain on Amazon's delivery network. Delivery times and customer reviews slipped. Problems were exacerbated by worker absences, and workers protested and even went on strike. Consequently, during the early months of COVID-19, Amazon's share of ecommerce actually fell. Walmart and Target benefited from Amazon's initial faltering. But, as the virus continued, Amazon spent billions stabilizing its supply chain, and its share of online commerce picked up again.

Ultimately, Amazon has been one of the biggest winners of the COVID-19 pandemic. In Q2 2020, Amazon made a record $88.9 billion in sales, showing double-digit revenue growth year over year.[9] Although the operations were weakened by the overdemand and pressure on the systems, the company made significant investments in logistics and delivery capabilities. For example, Amazon increased the number of delivery stations by 71%. Amazon's Q3 sales grew 37% year over year, while Q4 is predicted to grow from 28% to 38% year over year, with predicted sales between $112 billion and $121 billion.[10] Amazon CEO Jeff Bezos noted in his annual letter that although COVID-19 exerted a substantial strain on the company's systems, those stresses would ultimately help Amazon in the long run by forcing it to learn how to operate under chaos.

Amazon's Beginnings

Amazon started in 1995 as an online bookstore offering customers the opportunity to order books anytime, anywhere. Bezos chose the book industry specifically because the product could be digitalized so that the online assortment could be enormous—bigger, Bezos knew, than any physical store could ever match. Unlike other retail websites operating at the time, Amazon's website made "browsing" online as easy as browsing in a physical store.

The majority of the books were priced 10% to 30% cheaper than those sold at other stores, and customers did not pay sales tax for purchases made online. These advantages impressed customers and resulted in powerful word-of-mouth recommendations, which eventually spurred exponential growth. In December 1995, just 2,200 people had ever visited Amazon's webpage; today, Amazon sells substantially more than half of the books sold in the United States. From books, Amazon then moved on to other digitizable products, music, and DVDs. Amazon's success soon put many of the competing large big-box retailers, such as Borders, Tower Records, and Blockbuster, out of business.

Amazon Marketplace

In 2000, Amazon began allowing outside companies, including direct competitors (in terms of products sold), to sell on an Amazon open-ecommerce platform called Amazon Marketplace. Amazon collected a sales commission of up to 5% of each sale from these third-party sellers. In exchange, Amazon would deliver and store the product and allow consumers to buy products using Amazon's purchase technology.

Brands and other retailers including Toys "R" Us, Target, Circuit City, Gap, and Lands' End quickly signed on, only bolstering Amazon's grip on the marketplace. The program not only allowed Amazon to offer the largest assortment available online, but, as will be discussed later, also served to provide a sizable source of profit.

With this innovation, Amazon was soon selling every product from A to Z, as its logo promised. Amazon Marketplace now accounts for more than half of products sold on the Amazon platform.

Amazon Web Services

When working with the retailers on Amazon Marketplace, Amazon recognized that each merchant's IT application deployment required a long development process to build databases, computing, payment processing, and storage components. Each retailer had to start from scratch and go through similar processes, resulting in great inefficiencies.

Amazon then entered the Infrastructure as a Service (IaaS) business by utilizing the advantages of cloud computing and building up a reliable, scalable, and cost-efficient IT infrastructure called Amazon Web Services (AWS). Pricing was like a utility; users paid for what they used, thus avoiding costly upfront costs to build up systems.

AWS has been hugely successful. Small developers that could not afford upfront development costs signed on to AWS for cost-effective and reliable service. Large companies like General Electric also began to rent computing from Amazon. By 2015, AWS was servicing more than 1 million customers in 190 countries. It quickly became the dominant player in the space, with revenues larger than all of its competitors combined. AWS today offers over 70 IT services, including networking, storage, and analytics.

In 2018, Amazon controlled more than a third of the cloud market, more than twice the share of its next-closest competitor (Microsoft).[11] However, the space is getting more competitive, and Microsoft's share is growing, as are the shares of other competitors like Google and Oracle.

Plotting Amazon's Retailing Strategy

Amazon is definitely more than just a retailing company; it is also a true force in logistics, consumer technology, cloud computing, and digital advertising. It also sells products such as the Alexa personal assistant, the Kindle, and movies and television shows through its Prime Video platform. But its many moving parts work together to reinforce its dominant position in retailing—and that is the perspective that I will focus on. Although retailing is not the most profitable part of the business, it is Amazon's primary source of revenue. Using the Kahn Retailing Success Matrix framework, a leadership strategy requires the firm to be the market leader in one quadrant, build on that advantage to achieve leadership in a second quadrant, and then maintain fair value in the other two quadrants. Amazon seems to be following this prescription. It is clearly the market leader in the Frictionless quadrant. It builds on that advantage to be the market leader in a second quadrant (Low Price). Finally, Amazon is ready to provide at least fair value on customer expectations in the remaining two quadrants (Product Brand and Experiential).

Specifically, as figure 2.1 shows, in the Frictionless quadrant Amazon is pushing consumers' expectations higher and higher and constantly finds itself ahead of the pack. Other retailers scramble to keep up as Amazon keeps investing in developing innovations that allow it to continually leapfrog the competition.

In the Low Price quadrant, Amazon's strategy is to fiercely compete and to offer the lowest price possible. Amazon subsidizes thin margins in its retail transactions by leveraging profitability in other parts of its business, such as AWS, Marketplace, Amazon Prime, and more recently digital advertising.

In the Product Brand quadrant, Amazon is not a leader, but it strives to offer products and brands consumers want on its platform. In addition, Amazon tries to mitigate other brands' advantages by convincing consumers that those brands' premium prices are not warranted. This is illustrated on the matrix by showing the movement of the fair-value line downward toward the origin in this quadrant. This, then, allows Amazon to compete effectively either with its own brands or with those offered on Amazon Marketplace.

Finally, in the enhanced customer Experiential quadrant, Amazon is currently below fair value because of its emphasis on convenience

Figure 2.1. Plotting Amazon on the Kahn Retailing Success Matrix

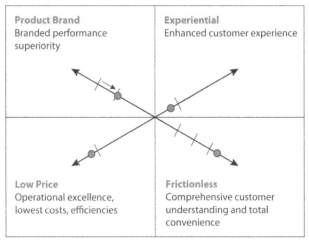

Explicitly trying to commoditize brands and products through strategies on its platform

Purchase of Whole Foods and new store concepts (e.g., Amazon Go) increasing physical footprint

Product Brand
Branded performance superiority

Experiential
Enhanced customer experience

Low Price
Operational excellence, lowest costs, efficiencies

Frictionless
Comprehensive customer understanding and total convenience

Offers low prices by minimizing margins; profitability comes elsewhere

Continues to shape customer expectations here; continuous innovations

rather than pleasurable experiences. Even with the purchase of Whole Foods and its opening of new Amazon stores, Amazon seems only to be reaching for fair value in this quadrant. These strategies are plotted in figure 2.1 and will be discussed in more detail in the next sections.

Key Leadership Position: Frictionless, Pain-Free Customer Experience

> *At Amazon, we are committed to being the most customer-centric company on Earth.*
> —Amazon.com

Amazon's defining leadership strategy is to be the best in the world in the Frictionless quadrant, and it achieves this by constantly innovating and raising customer expectations as to what it means to enjoy a convenient, seamless shopping experience. Amazon is laser focused on customer experience, specifically in terms of eliminating any pain points and proactively giving customers what they desire.

One of Amazon's earliest innovations, 1-Click, was introduced in 1997, and it serves as a metaphor for Amazon's overarching philosophy that shopping should be as easy and convenient as possible. 1-Click shopping meant that once consumers had entered their personal payment information, they did not have to enter it again; one click on the desired item would purchase it. This idea was so novel at the time that Amazon was awarded a US patent for the technology (notably, the patent expired in 2017). It is hard now to imagine that this was a patentable idea, but at the time, retailers typically strategized to keep consumers on their websites and in their stores longer (remember milk in the back of the store?) to try to maximize spend.

Amazon's hugely popular loyalty program, Amazon Prime, which offers free delivery and a large array of entertainment possibilities, gives the company another opportunity for success in this quadrant by providing the ability to collect customer data that can be used to fulfill customers' current and future needs. Finally, the always forward-looking Amazon is aiming to be a leader in the burgeoning world of the "connected home." With the introduction of Amazon Echo and Alexa, Amazon has developed another source of data and opportunities that will allow it to interact with consumers.

Best Loyalty Program: Amazon Prime

In 2005 Amazon launched its loyalty program, Amazon Prime. Prime members get free delivery and a plethora of entertainment options, including Instant Video, the Kindle Lending Library, Prime Music, Prime Drive, and Prime Photo. Other benefits include free grocery delivery, one free ebook a month, and access to streaming media content including new Amazon content. In addition, Prime members have access to Amazon's best price deals. All of these factors make Amazon Prime members exceedingly loyal. The program also provides Amazon with many touchpoints with the consumer each day, providing more and more data.

Amazon aggressively recruits new customers to become Prime members. In 2015, Amazon created Prime Day to celebrate its 20th anniversary. During this one-day-only event, Prime members were offered hugely discounted items. The event generated 86.3 million visits; for comparison, the company saw 87.1 million visits on Black Friday and 95.3 million visits on Cyber Monday during the same time period.

Strategies such as this continue to help Amazon attract new Prime customers, and as of January 2020 the company had 150 million subscribers worldwide. Some analysts speculate that as many as 82% of all American households have at least one Prime account.[12] This is important because Prime members spend 40% to 68% more money on Amazon's site than nonmembers, with the higher percentages occurring for customers who have been members longer. Amazon Prime membership also encourages much more frequent shopping. According to one survey by an independent consumer research firm, 95% of Prime members planned to renew their membership, and renewed members spend more in the subsequent year.[13] Bezos calls Prime the company's "flywheel"—a device used in engines to provide constant energy. Prime keeps customers loyal to Amazon and accelerates their purchasing, and this ever-spinning engine primes other aspects of the business.

Strategic Use of Data

Amazon's algorithms help provide personalized communications and recommendations for customers, and its detailed search filters help those customers find exactly what they want, when they want it. The more customers Amazon entices to Prime, the more likely sellers are to sign on to Marketplace and to use AWS. As a result, Amazon not only has an extensive dataset on how consumers search, purchase, and consume, but it also has data from its Marketplace that show how sellers sell, and from AWS it learns how developers create their infrastructure and retailing support systems. With this information, Amazon can not only provide the best recommendations for consumers but also use state-of-the-art innovations to maximize logistics and technology-enriched environments. This strategy of getting data from all sources, then leveraging this information to get smarter products that entice more consumers and sellers to Amazon's site, is yet another example of the classic flywheel model. The other huge advantage of these data is to provide the information to advertisers, another huge source of revenue. In addition to understanding what people buy, Amazon knows where people live, what credit cards they use, what media they watch, and what healthcare products they purchase.

Connected Home: Amazon Echo and IoT

Underlying the fast-growing world of the Internet of Things (IoT) is the idea that computers and other digital devices can transfer data over a network without requiring human-to-human or human-to-computer interaction. We are in the early stages of this burgeoning market, but Amazon has begun to lay the groundwork for dominance.

A major emphasis in the IoT, or connected home space, is the growing focus on voice assistants that allow for a customer-centric purchase journey right in the home. Amazon's entry here is the Amazon Echo, a voice-enabled wireless speaker that answers to commands beginning with the word "Alexa." If Amazon can get Echo in the majority of US homes, it will become the dominant platform for natural language processing interaction—connecting the home, wearables, and even the car dashboard.

A recent survey shows that Amazon is the leader of the market for voice-activated smart speakers, with a share of 53%.[14] But its lead continues to decline, as it is facing tough competition from Google (Home), which partnered with Walmart, and Apple's HomePod. The same survey showed Google's share to be 31%.

An eMarketer report predicts that 21.6 million people will have purchased a smart speaker by the end of 2020 and that 10.8% of US digital consumers will buy goods this year using the smart speaker.[15] This penetration of purchasing via smart speaker is lower than analysts had initially predicted. Consumers are more likely to use their smart speakers to listen to audio and to make inquiries. Speculation is that the slow adoption of using this technology for purchasing is because of consumers' fears about payment security and privacy. People also cannot see what they are purchasing unless there is a screen connected with the smart speaker, so most ordering has been for repeat purchases.

Investigations of Anticompetitive Behavior

Amazon's use of all these data sources, including data from its competition, has caused concerns about violations of antitrust policies. Specifically, regulators are concerned about Amazon's dual role as both the operator of the marketplace and the cloud *and* a competitor. Amazon maintains that it does not abuse its power and size, and its policies state that it does not use information from its competitors. However, a *Wall Street Journal* investigation found that Amazon employees used data from other sellers to develop competing products, and that this information is frequently used to help Amazon decide how to price an item.[16] The United States (the Justice Department, Federal Trade Commission, and Congress) has been probing into Amazon's alleged anticompetitive behavior, as has the European Union.

For its part, Nate Sutton, associate general counsel at Amazon, specifically testified in front of Congress that Amazon doesn't "use individual seller data directly to compete."[17] Defenders of Amazon's policies note that retailers frequently create store brands to compete with national brands and rely on retail data that they obtain to create, position, and price those store brands. However, the amount of data Amazon can obtain is much more comprehensive and extensive.

Building on Customer Centricity to Become a Low-Price Leader

Everybody wants . . . low prices. . . . That is something that is universally desired all over the world.
—Jeff Bezos

Amazon is definitely a low-price leader, both for its own brands and for outside brands offered on its site. Amazon can afford to trim margins on its own brands because retail transactions are not its critical profit generator. Rather, profit generation comes through its AWS, Amazon Prime, digital advertising, and Amazon Marketplace initiatives. Amazon Marketplace generates profits through the pockets of the company's competitors, while Prime generates profits through subscription fees and increased purchasing from loyal members. The low-price strategies encouraged through Amazon's strategies described in this chapter (in addition to the superb customer service and convenience) keep Amazon's customers addicted to the site.

In addition to promoting pricing strategies that encourage intense price competition, Amazon also works to improve margins by efficiency in its cost structure. This is accomplished through Amazon's automated fulfillment centers that can efficiently and quickly move product from warehouses to where they need to be delivered (by plane or cargo trucks).

Profits from Other Services: AWS, Marketplace, Digital Advertising, Prime

Rather than trying to make significant profit on each retail transaction (according to one expert I spoke with, Amazon has 3% margins on its merchandise transactions), Amazon is profitable through four mechanisms: (1) AWS; (2) Amazon Prime, which provides Amazon with revenues through a subscription model and increased spending; (3) Amazon Marketplace; and (4) digital advertising. (In 2019,

Morgan Stanley estimated the worth of Amazon's advertising business at $125 billion.)[18]

AWS is the engine behind Amazon's profits, as it provides much-desired server capacity to small retailers and startups. It is Amazon's most profitable business, and in 2018 it generated $25 billion in sales. Investopedia estimated that as of October 2020, AWS generated 63% of Amazon's operating income.[19]

Through Amazon Prime, meanwhile, the company generates revenue in two ways. First, of course, members pay a fee to join Prime. In 2020, the Amazon Prime membership cost $119 per year, or $12.99 per month. In addition, Amazon Prime members spend an average of $1,400 per year on the Amazon shopping platform, compared with $600 per year for non-Prime shoppers, according to a survey conducted by Statista in March 2019.[20]

Amazon Marketplace also generates operating profit, even though Amazon does not own any of the products sold there. The platform also gives Amazon insight into its competitors' transactions. For these third-party sales, Amazon charges fees and does not have to take on inventory risks. In 2020, these sales represented more than half of Amazon's total revenue.

To further serve third-party sellers, Amazon offers Fulfillment by Amazon (FBA), where vendors (for a fee, of course) can use Amazon's fulfillment centers for warehousing, order fulfillment, logistics, and customer service. These products are then allowed to be offered to Amazon's Prime customers. It costs third-party sellers *more* to sell on Amazon with FBA than on eBay. However, more logistics options are available, and even accounting for the higher fees, Amazon's business with third-party sellers is growing.

Through investments in its fulfillment and delivery systems, Amazon has made it more difficult for merchants to ship products themselves and is forcing them to pay Amazon to do it. To fulfill customer expectations, Amazon requires third-party sellers to meet the new one- and two-day pledges that Amazon Prime guarantees. If sellers cannot meet these expectations, they lose the Prime fast-shipping label. Historically, these sellers relied on other shipping providers like UPS, FedEx, or USPS, but if those services cannot meet the Amazon-mandated guarantees, the third-party merchants are forced to use Amazon's own services. During the summer of 2020, Amazon delivered 66% of its own packages, up from 61% the preceding year. Some analysts are predicting that this figure will reach 80% by 2021.[21] Interestingly, both UPS and FedEx also saw year-over-year growth during this time (even during the economic slowdown), as COVID-19 accelerated consumers' practice of purchasing online and having orders delivered to their homes.

Amazon also generates revenue from advertising, and revenue growth is accelerating year over year. Amazon's strength comes from its ability to target consumers on its platforms using data from a variety of sources. The critical advantage, compared with advertising dollars spent on Google or Facebook, is that advertisers can provide ads right at the point of purchase. Some predictions suggest that Amazon could have a 14% share of US digital ad sales by 2023.[22]

Marketplace Tactics Drive Merchants to Lower-Price Strategies

In addition to being a profit generator, Amazon Marketplace also incentivizes merchants to lower prices. First, since Marketplace is an open platform, Amazon does not police it to make sure that diverted gray-market products are not included. Amazon's open platform allows almost anyone to create new product listings. Consequently, resellers can sell products unbeknownst to manufacturers, and the products may violate contracts. For example, third-party sellers typically buy legitimate products from retailers such as Walmart or T.J.Maxx, or even the brands' own outlets, and then offer those brands for sale on Amazon with slightly higher prices than they acquired them. These products can easily then be sold below minimum advertised prices— and may be sold under not-quite-legitimate brand names.

Second, if a product comes in at the most competitive price, it is labeled with Amazon's Buy Box, which will increase sales volume enormously, compensating for lower margins and providing more commission to Amazon. This encourages overall price competition among Amazon's competitors, which helps make Amazon the go-to lower-priced retailer.

Third, for product searches that occur on other search engines, Amazon buys display advertising for popular brands, then sends those consumers back to the Amazon site. Since Amazon has access to the third-party purchase transactions that occur on its site, it can make sure it features brands that have been shown to attract consumers. Once on the Amazon site, the customer is subject to Amazon algorithms and website priorities that encourage price competition. In addition, Amazon uses this information to offer its own lower-priced alternatives in the Amazon Basics program.

Another interesting strategy Amazon uses to ensure that it is able to offer the lowest prices is to partner with merchants in India that will be able to sell their goods directly to US consumers on the Amazon platform. Amazon is partnering with India behemoths like the Tata Group, as well as smaller sellers that can offer handcrafted goods. In addition to broadening its product line, Amazon can, via this new initiative, tack on large margins. Bezos has said he will prioritize India ecommerce as an avenue for growth for the future. At the same time, Amazon may be looking toward the Middle East: In 2017 it purchased Souq.com, known as the "Amazon of the Middle East." This potentially opens up Egypt, Saudi Arabia, and the United Arab Emirates to Amazon as well.

Finally, Amazon competes against the third-party merchants that sell on its platform with its own private brand called Amazon Basics. Many of the products in this category are sold only to Prime members. Again, since Amazon controls all the data, it has enormous insight into where there may be gaps for lower-priced brands and then produces those private-label products. Amazon currently has private-label brands in apparel, consumer packaged goods, and diapers. The company also makes it hard for other retailers to match its prices, as it has begun to use blocking technology so the retailers cannot see what is happening with regard to Amazon's branded product efforts.

Although Amazon publically denies inappropriate use of competitive data, the *New York Times* interviewed current Amazon employees, sellers, suppliers, and consultants to determine exactly how Amazon dictates prices for retailers doing business on its platform.[23] According to the *Times*, Amazon punishes businesses if the items are available for as little as a penny less elsewhere. There is pressure to use Amazon's warehouses and to purchase ads on the site. This makes it harder for retailers to make a profit on the Amazon platform. The amount Amazon collects from merchants has increased over the years.

In spite of these aggressive tactics designed to lower prices, brands and resellers are enticed to sell on Amazon Marketplace because they do not have to spend marketing dollars to drive traffic to their sites; Amazon's volume is bigger than any other ecommerce site. And 55% of product searches in the United States start on Amazon, as compared with 28% on other search engines such as Google. This number is even starker for Amazon Prime users, where 79% of product searches start on Amazon, compared with only 12% on Google.

Efficiency in Lowest-Cost Fulfillment: Amazon's Fulfillment Centers

Another way Amazon maintains its low-price structure is through cost containment. Amazon is on target to fulfill its mission of becoming a logistics and transport leader, which is key to retail dominance. It can make a wider range of products available and deliver those products faster than its competitors can. Some of this expertise in logistics has come from hiring a number of Walmart executives to leverage that retailer's expertise.

The demand for faster delivery times has necessitated that Amazon expand its footprint of fulfillment and distribution centers, building them closer to where the customer lives. Because Amazon does not have the physical-store presence of its competition, the company's leadership has been strategically locating its warehouses, expanding recently to allow same-day delivery to more customers.

Amazon has also recently received federal approval to use drones to deliver packages to its customers. The goal is to develop the technology so that drones will be fully integrated into the airspace to help deliver products. Amazon has stated that its vision for the future is to offer 30-minute delivery. Amazon currently offers same-day delivery in many of its markets.

Maintaining Fair Value in the Branded Products Quadrant

Your margin is my opportunity.
—One of Jeff Bezos's "best-known bon mots,"
according to the *Wall Street Journal*

While Amazon's critical leadership advantages are in the Frictionless and Low Price quadrants, it must maintain a credible presence in the Product Brand quadrant as well—offering at least fair value here. For sure, it is able to compete effectively by offering the largest breadth of assortment, and, as described, it has been able to bring in a significant number of branded products to its platform through Amazon Marketplace.

But producers of many of the most prestigious branded products (which consumers really covet) are loath to sell through Amazon, because they know they would be putting too much control into Amazon's hands. Amazon will dictate inventory, control the customer data, and set pricing. Although Amazon will sell some customer analytics to the brand, it will not release information on conversion rates and customer demographics. Further, Amazon's algorithms prioritize Amazon's goals—not the brands' goals.

Amazon's strategy does not help it to be the leader in offering prestigious, luxury brands. Rather, Bezos's strategy seems to be to try to commoditize those brands, then use Amazon Prime advantages to incentivize consumers to purchase from Amazon Basics (on price value) or from Amazon Marketplace, where website algorithms also encourage lower pricing, rather than having consumers purchase premium-priced branded goods from competitors. Brands' margins are Amazon's opportunity. And again, this was plotted on the matrix by showing movement of the fair-value line toward the origin.

Goal to Offer Largest Breadth of Assortment; Brands' Equity Often Diminished as a Result

To offer the largest assortment, Amazon has a variety of inducements to encourage third-party retailers to use Amazon. Amazon does not police its offerings, and so these third-party sellers may be selling branded products in ways that are not appreciated by the brands themselves. More and more, Amazon is being charged with a "kind of lawlessness," as the *New York Times* has called it.[24] A *Wall Street Journal* investigation found that thousands of products on Amazon's marketplace were declared unsafe by federal agencies.[25]

Amazon has a hands-off approach to many issues related to the legitimacy of products sold on its platform and fake reviews, typically being reactive rather than proactive in dealing with customer complaints. Amazon's position has historically been that it is the retailers' responsibility to ensure products conform to copyright, trademark, privacy, or other guarantees.

Given Amazon's strategies, it is clear that while Amazon may be customer-centric, it is not competitor-merchant friendly—even though these merchants are incentivized to sell on the Amazon platform because of the sheer volume of users. But, when merchants sell on Amazon, they don't own their own data; they are always incentivized to compete on price (thus cannibalizing their own potentially higher-margin business that could have come through direct selling or through selling on other retailers' platforms); and they can't offer a customized high-touch customer experience, which is crucial to some brands' cachet.

With more media attention to the issue of counterfeits and with more consumers experiencing subpar quality or counterfeit products they have purchased on Amazon Marketplace, Amazon has been forced to respond to what has become more of a customer-benefit issue. Amazon has declared it will spend billions of dollars to police the products on its site and in 2020 announced it will set up a Counterfeit Crimes Unit. This unit will bring together former federal prosecutors, investigators, and data analysts to work with brands to find the culprits, litigate, and help law enforcement officials fight criminal actions.

Why Do Some Brands Agree to Sell on Amazon?

Given Amazon's strategies to promote lower and lower prices, why would retailers or brands sell on Amazon Marketplace in the first place? If the brand is small enough, getting access to Amazon's volume is attractive, as is avoiding spending marketing dollars to drive traffic to its own site. For very small brands, this may be the only way for them to get scale.

But even big retailers like Toys "R" Us have been attracted to Amazon—and ultimately suffered for the relationship. In 2000, Amazon and Toys "R" Us signed a 10-year partnership that made Amazon the exclusive online retailer for Toys "R" Us products. Amazon designed the website and assisted in warehouse, fulfillment, and customer service. Customers who went to the Toys "R" Us website put their orders into an Amazon shopping cart.

Why did Toys "R" Us do this? Apparently, it had the mistaken impression that it would be the exclusive provider of toys for Amazon. But Amazon had other ideas, as it also partnered with Target and other independent third-party sellers to sell toys. Toys "R" Us filed a lawsuit against Amazon, and in 2006 a judge ordered the dissolution of the partnership. Amazon was deemed to have broken the contract but was not forced to pay any damages, and it continued to have success in the toy business. Toys "R" Us, on the other hand, subsequently failed playing catch-up. In 2017, it declared bankruptcy.

Amazon is ruthless in leveraging its connections and competing against branded products that are popular with its customers— and many times brands are helpless to stop Amazon. In 2017, Amazon went up against Lululemon by using a top Lululemon supplier, Eclat

Textile, to make private-label athletic clothing for Amazon. Although Lulu has some patents, most of them focus on design features and not fabric technology. Lulu's share price dropped two days after the news.

Amazon has also been relentless in competing against book publishers in its quest to cater to its customers' interests. For example, Amazon makes it easy for consumers to choose to buy a used book rather than a new book by making them seem virtually the same. However, when the consumer chooses to buy the used book, the publisher makes nothing—but Amazon does. The value of the used book, though, is a function of the investment the publisher and the author made in producing the original content. Under Amazon's model, there is no royalty or any profit stream from reselling.

The situation has gotten more extreme during COVID-19, which has radically shifted the retailing environment. Now, even brands with strong equity have had to rely more on Amazon, with fewer alternatives amid more physical-store closings. This is not uniquely an Amazon advantage: As with much of the repercussions from the pandemic, bigger retailers like Amazon, Walmart, and Target are benefiting as smaller companies suffer.

Moving into Fashion

If consumers still see value in premium/luxury brands—and if these brands can manage not to sell on Amazon's platform—Amazon will be at a disadvantage in this quadrant. Amazon is potentially vulnerable here, suggesting that this could be a viable way for retailers to compete. I will discuss this more in subsequent chapters, which describe luxury brands' and digitally native brands' strategies. For Amazon's purposes, it is an area the company must eventually shore up.

Given this potential vulnerability, Amazon is building a fashion luxury platform and will try to entice the best European and US brands to sell there. Its approach is to offer a marketplace model and allow brands selling on the platform to have access to Amazon's centralized warehousing and delivery network. Fashion-loving customers coming to Amazon will be directed to a fashion platform to which only wholesale vendors have access (not resellers or third-party sellers). Brands that sell on this platform have better control of their brand identity, the look and feel of their virtual stores, and the fashion pages where specific brands can be easily accessed, while third-party sellers are relegated to regular results pages where customers have to search through hundreds of pages of results. There are plans to work with the brands on TV, film, and streaming projects as well. Although there has been continual reluctance from the big luxury and fashion retailers to engage with Amazon, with these new strategies and the negative repercussions from the pandemic crisis, Amazon has begun to win over fashion brands including Calvin Klein, Tommy Hilfiger, and Michael Kors and designers including Anna Sui Tahkoon, Tabitha Simmons, Derek Lam, and Batsheva. If Amazon can fight against counterfeits and give the brands the ability to manage their own customers' experiences, it may find more acceptance.

Amazon's Move into Healthcare and Grocery

With the purchase of Whole Foods and other food stores, and the acceleration to ecommerce shopping for grocery due to COVID-19, Amazon is clearly a player in the grocery business. Amazon increased its grocery delivery capacity by more than 160% and tripled pickup spots for grocery during the pandemic. Although there were some initial hiccups when Amazon picked up the slack for online grocery and delivery demand, Amazon's investments clearly paid off. A summer 2020 Grocery Shopping Study conducted by the Retail Feedback Group showed that Amazon had the highest ratings for customer satisfaction among a sample of 2,000 online grocery shoppers. The survey showed that 36% of respondents said they were first-time online shoppers, and 52% of the shoppers said they would do more shopping with Amazon in the future.[26]

In August 2020, Amazon announced its first physical Amazon Fresh grocery store. This store has cashierless and more traditional checkouts and offers a seamless grocery experience that links online and offline shopping. It also uses Alexa features to help shoppers navigate the store. The assortment of grocery products includes national and private brands, including those from Amazon and Whole Foods. Opening in 2020, it features pandemic safety measures, including daily temperature checks and face masks for all employees, and requires face coverings for customers.

Amazon is also moving steadily into healthcare. Amazon acquired online pharmacy PillPack in June 2019 and is planning to move into the pharmacy market, where speculation is that it will enter the specialty drug market (competitors here include CVS, Walgreens, and Express Scripts). PillPack distributes pills for customers with chronic conditions as well as customers with multiple prescriptions—and more important, PillPack has pharmacy licenses in all 50 states and relationships with the major pharmacy benefit managers like Express Scripts and CVS Health.

Amazon may also investigate health-tech opportunities like telemedicine or electronic medical records. This is currently a splintered space, but if Amazon could put together a platform that would attract all of these different apps in one place, the result would be powerful. Even putting aside Amazon's relative lack of experience in healthcare, it would bring a novel customer-centric perspective to that arena.

Amazon has also partnered with Berkshire Hathaway and JPMorgan Chase and launched the joint venture now known as Haven in an effort to pool collective resources to control the rise in health costs and concentrate on health insurance. They may also look into the healthcare distribution channel, where three companies, AmerisourceBergen, McKesson, and Cardinal Health, account for the majority of revenue.

Finally, Amazon may enter the primary care market. In September 2019, Amazon Care was introduced to its employees in Seattle. Amazon Care is a virtual and in-person clinic. Amazon is partnering with Oasis Medical, a family practice clinic, to provide the service.

Competing in Physical Retailing

*We see our customers as invited guests to a party, and we
are the hosts. It's our job every day to make every important
aspect of the customer experience a little bit better.*
—Jeff Bezos

In the Experiential quadrant, Amazon has historically been absent, having started as an online retailer and prioritizing technology over a physical-store experience. Even though there has been incredible growth in ecommerce sales, most industry experts believe there will always be a role for the brick-and-mortar store. So, although Amazon is much further behind other more traditional retailers in this quadrant, it has been experimenting with different store formats. In addition, it recently purchased Whole Foods and partnered with Kohl's for product returns, and there are constant rumors of similar new partnerships.

In implementing its physical-store strategies, Amazon seems to be less focused on providing superlative, pleasurable, positive experiential store experiences and more focused on adding a physical presence to its frictionless shopping experience. By building and acquiring physical stores, Amazon acknowledges that brick and mortar still holds value for many customers who want to "touch and feel" the product, want goods immediately, or want to interact in a social environment. However, Amazon's priority is to find innovative ways to integrate the online/offline experience into one seamless whole.

Amazon's Own Stores

Amazon has built several branded bookstores that sell books with high customer ratings and showcase the company's growing family of gadgets. On the surface these outlets look like regular bookstores. But there is an important difference: When you shop in an Amazon bookstore, you have to access the Amazon app. None of the books in the store have prices shown; to learn the price, or to see reviews, consumers have to log in to the app while in the store and hold their phones up to the book or UPC code. This allows Amazon to connect online behavior with behavior in the store, to offer more information about the books, to charge different prices to Prime and non-Prime customers, and to continue to collect customer data.

Amazon has also opened a number of small grocery or convenience stores called Amazon Go, which again teach consumers to shop with their phones using the Amazon app. Amazon Go stores use mobile ecommerce and RFID tech, machine learning, and computer vision to allow customers to shop without having to stand in line waiting for a cashier. In these stores, consumers swipe into the store with their phones. Their purchases are recorded by sensors and cameras that transmit information about the customers' movements and actions, and also about which products are ultimately chosen, to an online processing system. When customers leave the store, charges are automatically assigned to customers' Amazon Prime accounts.

Amazon has expanded Amazon Go grocery stores into California, Massachusetts, Colorado, New York, and Washington, DC. Amazon is also in talks to bring its "just walk out" cashierless technology to airports, baseball stadiums, and movie theaters.

Amazon's Purchase of Whole Foods

With the purchase of Whole Foods, Amazon has taken control of urban real estate and grocery outlets, which can double as Amazon warehouses and help Amazon more conveniently deliver to the last mile. These 450 stores are predominantly located in upper-income, prime location areas that can also serve as distribution nodes for everything Amazon sells. Reports indicate that Amazon may bring its cashierless tech found at its Go convenience stores to Whole Foods markets by 2021.

Amazon has made a number of changes since acquiring Whole Foods. First, Prime members are offered special prices and delivery options at Whole Foods. Amazon has also increased online options and selectively slashed prices on certain items. According to Gordon Haskett Research Advisors, a standard basket of goods at Whole Foods has dropped in price by about 2.5% since the acquisition.[27] Whole Foods items are now also available on Amazon. As mentioned earlier, Amazon is also in the early stages of a separate grocery entry called Fresh.

Since the advent of COVID-19, Amazon has invested more in Whole Foods. It hired more than 75,000 employees to fill surging demand and launched a new feature that gives customers a way to schedule time to shop and get a virtual place in line for delivery options. Curbside pickup options also doubled from roughly 80 stores to 150.[28] As Amazon becomes more invested in grocery, more changes are expected.

Conclusion

As figure 2.1 makes clear, Amazon is the undisputed leader in the Frictionless quadrant and is continually innovating to hold this position well into the future. Its mantra is "They who control the data control the world," and Prime serves as the flywheel to make it happen. Using its clout, it has pushed retail prices lower and lower, giving it the leadership position in the Low Price quadrant as well.

Currently in the Product Brand quadrant, Amazon offers the largest assortments but is not quite at fair value on branded, prestigious products. Its strategy here seems to be twofold: first, to do what it can to mitigate other brands' advantages, and second, to follow up with a branded luxury/fashion platform of its own. Finally, in the Experiential quadrant, Amazon has acknowledged the continued importance of physical stores. Its strategy here, though, is to build customer experience based on frictionless shopping rather than high-end luxurious experiential interaction.

To see evidence that Jeff Bezos planned this strategy from the start, search online for the term "Amazon's Virtuous Cycle." You will see a graphic that Jeff Bezos is reported to have drawn on a napkin when he started the business in the late 1990s. This graphic suggests that growth will come as a result of "customer experience," which will drive traffic to the site, which in turn will attract sellers to the site, which in turn will provide a very large selection of products, which will lead right back to a better customer experience. Then once that cycle is complete, Amazon can leverage that advantage to lower its cost structure and thus continue to lower prices, which again will lead back to a better customer experience. Amazon is the undisputed catalyst for massive changes in retailing, and the strategy has remained the same for the last 30 years.

Chapter 3

Price Leadership Is Not Enough
Successful "Everyday Low Price" Retailers Add Frictionless Expertise

In This Chapter: Kahn Retailing Success Strategy
- Key Leadership Strength: "Always Low Prices"
- Secondary Leadership Strength: Building a Frictionless Omnichannel Experience
- Fair Value in Branded Product and Experiential

Walmart was founded by Sam Walton in 1962 with the motto "Always low prices" (later changed to "Save money. Live better."). Walmart stocked a wide range of products, its stores stayed open longer than those of the competition, and it guaranteed the lowest prices. Although margins were low, it sold large quantities— and made big profits.

When a Walmart store came into a region, other competitors suffered. Historically, its model of "operational excellence" made it the world's most streamlined distributor of goods. It replaced the "high-low" pricing strategies of many grocery stores with an EDLP strategy that helped it manage inventory much more efficiently and keep costs down.

As Walmart's sales grew, its power grew, and this dynamic changed how companies in its supply chain did business with it. This in turn provided Walmart further advantages. Walmart became so important in consumer goods that firms like Procter & Gamble built offices near Bentonville, Arkansas, Walmart's headquarters. When

Walmart set goals, manufacturers found ways to meet them. For example, Walmart could persuade its product manufacturers to change the size of their packaging or guarantee the lowest prices in any region for any good it sold simply because it had the power to make these demands of its suppliers.

The Strategic Advantages of an EDLP Strategy

Why did this lowest-price strategy work so well?

There are three reasons. First, some consumers will always value a good deal. Second, many consumers are genuinely price sensitive and living within a budget. For these shoppers, price is the most important criterion for choosing a retailer. Finally, there are people who believe, as Jeff Bezos does, that brands are overpriced and that most products are basically commodities. So why pay more?

Following this strategy, Walmart grew so big that today it is estimated that 90% of Americans live within 10 miles of one of its stores. Walmart is still the largest retailer in the world, with $514.4 billion in global revenue in fiscal year 2019, despite Amazon having a larger market capitalization.[29]

Walmart's leadership strategy continues to be one of low prices. But in the competitive world of retailing, having the lowest price is no longer enough. Amazon has changed the playing field, and frictionless shopping is the norm. Walmart has had to pivot to a second leadership advantage, providing consumers with a frictionless omnichannel strategy. COVID-19 has only accelerated this need. But Walmart is fighting back. During Q2 of 2020, smack in the middle of the pandemic, Walmart's same-store sales in the United States rose 9.3%, and its online sales for the three-month period ending in June grew 97%.[30]

There will always be other low-price retailers that can threaten Walmart's position. Target, although significantly smaller than Amazon and Walmart, is successfully attracting consumers with its low-price strategy as well as clever merchandising and pleasurable in-store experiences. Aldi, a German discounter that claims it can offer the lowest price, competes mostly through private-label goods.

Costco is also a big player in the low-price segment, and I will discuss its strategy in chapter 6. And there are the dollar stores, such as Dollar General, that continue to invest in brick-and-mortar retail, although they cater to a different demographic.

How Can Walmart Compete?

Walmart has had to augment its strategy, because relying only on low prices as its advantage is no longer sufficient. It must deliver to a second leadership value: frictionless. It also has to deliver at fair value in the other two quadrants of brand and experience as its competition ramps up customers' expectations.

One sustainable differential advantage that Walmart continues to enjoy, especially vis-à-vis Amazon, is its large number of stores and its highly efficient operations and logistics. This provides a competitive edge over purely online merchants, because store locations offer the opportunity for quick last-minute delivery or in-store pickup. Walmart is also expert at the complexities of handling perishable items.

Its other clear advantage is its sheer number of sales associates; it is the largest private employer in the United States. Recently, understanding the importance of this asset, the company has invested more in its employees, raising salary levels, improving working conditions, and reorganizing its workforce to better fit the needs of the modern-day customer.

Walmart's Bold New Strategy

Walmart purchased Jet.com for $3.3 billion in August 2016 with the dual aim of positioning the company for faster ecommerce growth and creating a seamless omnichannel shopping experience. The company chose Jet.com because it was one of the fastest-growing and most innovative ecommerce companies in the United States, cofounded by the forward-thinking Marc Lore, who previously cofounded Quidsi, the parent company of ecommerce sites Diapers.com, Soap.com, and Wag.com. As part of the deal, Lore was enlisted to run Walmart .com as president and CEO.

The purchase and integration of Jet.com brought with it a more upscale and millennial audience that would complement Walmart's core older base. Jet had also demonstrated an ability to scale quickly, had best-in-class technology, and had already attracted more than 2,400 retailers and brand partners to its platform.

As Walmart built up its ecommerce experience, it also leveraged its physical-store advantages as part of the deal. For example, as Walmart initially ramped up its ecommerce experience, it offered lower prices to consumers who were willing to order online but pick up in the store. Essentially, with this option, consumers bear the costs of the "last mile delivery" (which is often the most expensive part of the overall delivery costs), and in return, share in those savings. The strategy worked. In the first year under Lore's leadership, Walmart's ecommerce sales rose 63%, with a 60% rise in digital gross merchandise volume. Its same-store sales increased 1.4%, and traffic to those stores rose 1.5%.[31]

The integration of Jet.com built on Walmart's historical low-price leadership model helped it gain real advantages in the Frictionless quadrant, allowing the retailer to offer an omnichannel experience. Reflecting this radical change in strategy, Walmart announced on February 1, 2017, that it would be changing its name from Wal-Mart Stores, Inc., to Walmart Inc.

Plotting Walmart's Strategy on the Kahn Retailing Success Matrix

Since 2016, after the purchase of Jet.com, Walmart has invested significantly in its ecommerce business, and its digital revenues grew from $10 billion in 2016 to over $41 billion in 2020. Walmart's US ecommerce sales have risen from 2% of total sales to 8% (right before COVID-19 hit the United States in January 2020). Projections following the pandemic are expected to be as high as 12% of total sales.[32]

Walmart has learned, however, that it does better as a single-entity retailer than as a retailer with disparate parts. It has recently discontinued the platform Jet.com and folded its entire ecommerce ecosystem into Walmart.com. The website has been completely overhauled and now offers a state-of-the-art online experience.

Walmart's strategy in the Frictionless quadrant is to build the best omnichannel experience, and a key to its growth is to leverage both the ecommerce ecosystem and its physical stores. It has been using its stores as mini online fulfillment centers and creating new customer-friendly options like "buy online, pick up in the store" (BOPIS). Walmart can also deliver food within 10 miles of a store to 90% of the US population, and can do it faster and cheaper than anyone else. Finally, Walmart has recently announced its own loyalty program, Walmart+, which offers free delivery for purchases over $35.

As Walmart continues to show strength in the Frictionless quadrant, it will also continue to invest in the Product Brand quadrant. The company plans to build up its own marketplace options and to develop private brands that will move Walmart to fair value or possibly above in this quadrant. Finally, in the Experiential quadrant, with its consideration of purchasing a minority stake in TikTok (regardless of whether that materializes), Walmart has signaled it understands the importance of social commerce and engaging younger generations.

These strategies are plotted in figure 3.1. First is the straightforward plotting of Walmart's historical strength in the Low Price quadrant and its emerging strength in the Frictionless quadrant. I have added arrows in the other two quadrants, Product Brand and Experiential, to represent the strategies announced (but not completely implemented) to meet or exceed expectations. Hence, I have plotted Walmart currently below expectations in the Product Brand and Experiential quadrants because even as it is rapidly investing in these quadrants, the expectations are continuing to grow due to the fierce competition.

Figure 3.1. Plotting Walmart on the Kahn Retailing Success Matrix

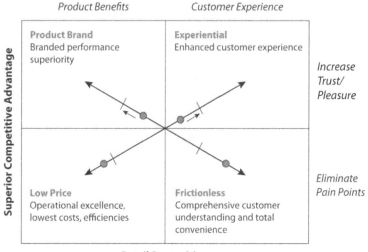

Investing for the Future in the Frictionless Quadrant

Faster, Better Delivery Options

Walmart is competing successfully in the Frictionless quadrant by leveraging the advantages its stores offer. Walmart has been growing its curbside pickup since 2014, but during the pandemic it has accelerated the initiative. Walmart trains employees to carefully select meat and produce options to meet customer demands. The company has also developed automated vending machines to retrieve online orders. On the home delivery front, Walmart has enhanced its options by using first-party and third-party services, such as a partnership with Instacart.

In the middle of 2020, Walmart announced its new membership service, Walmart+, which guarantees free shipping on tens of thousands of items, including produce and groceries. Priced under Amazon Prime's $119 at $98 a year, the new membership service requires a minimum order of $35 to qualify for free shipping. Unlike Prime, Walmart's service does not include streaming entertainment.

Stores Converted to Warehouses

To excel in the Frictionless quadrant, Walmart has leveraged advantages from its stores. For example, Walmart has converted some store space into warehouse facilities that store items for delivery. Some Sam's Clubs have been transformed into ecommerce fulfillment centers. Although the process has been accelerated during the pandemic, it has been in progress since 2017, when 60 retail operations had entered at least the preplanning stages of being transitioned to industrial use.

As much as possible, ecommerce fulfillment processes in existing stores have been automated. For example, in some of the backrooms of the Walmart stores, there are floor-to-ceiling robotic systems from which workers can assemble online orders. Robots then carry small baskets along metal tracks to collect the items, which can later be bagged for either pickup or delivery. The backroom automated systems are an attempt to solve two problems: labor costs and aisle congestion. An automated system is also better for inventory control and monitoring stock-outs. Using the stores as fulfillment centers offers a critical advantage because they are close to where the customers live. As of January 2020, Walmart offered home grocery delivery from more than 1,000 stores.

Internet of Things

Walmart has also invested in the connected home platform and voice technology. In August 2017 it partnered with Google to offer its customers the ability to order hundreds of thousands of products by voice. Although other retailers such as Target, Costco, and Ulta work with Google to sell products through Google Express, only Walmart is allowed access to the voice-enabled network. Walmart shoppers can link Walmart accounts to Google Express and can then order through voice or on Google Home or by shopping on Google Express. Their past-purchase histories will be accessible to facilitate the process.

Growth in Product Brand

Initially, after acquiring Jet.com, Walmart worked with Lore to buy up digitally native vertical brands (DNVBs) both to build bigger assortments that fill out the "long tail" and to add more prestigious items that appeal to different demographic groups. Some of these acquisitions have since been sold off, and Walmart has looked to different strategies, which will be described below, to fulfill these two goals.

The company's initial strategy under Lore was to try to lure the younger, affluent, and digitally savvy shoppers to Walmart through the acquisition of digitally native brands and the startup Jet Black, which was a shop-by-text service for more affluent shoppers. Over time, Walmart has divested some of these early acquisitions and closed down the Jet Black shop-by-text service.

Walmart has also added to its assortment through its own private-label brands. The company has historically had three of the top-selling private-label brands in its stores: Equate, Great Value, and Sam's Choice. Doug McMillon, CEO of Walmart, reported that Walmart's private brands were growing faster than its overall sales. The largest private brand, Great Value, has more than $27 billion in revenues per year globally.[33]

Building Bigger Assortments

To build larger assortments, Walmart has mirrored both Amazon and its partner in China, JD.com. It has augmented its marketplace platform by adding third-party sellers to its online store. In the past four years, more than 45,000 retailers have been added. When Walmart acquired Jet.com, it had only about 3 million items in its online assortment, but in 2020 that assortment numbered around 40 million.

Walmart also partnered with Shopify, a company that helps small businesses set up online stores from scratch. Walmart has announced it would add 1,200 of Shopify's best merchants by the end of 2020, with more merchants likely to follow in the future.[34] These new sellers will be able to synchronize their assortments with Walmart.com and use its logistics tools to track inventory and fulfillment.

Adding Prestige Brands

Walmart has always been known as a low-price retailer and efficient operator, but these labels have hampered its reputation as a fashion brand. As its aspirations grow, Walmart is now focusing on attracting more fashion-minded consumers to its site and stores.

Denise Incandela, head of fashion for US ecommerce for Walmart .com, has made it her mission to make Walmart a shopping destination for fashion. Rather than following Lore's strategy to purchase hip digitally native brands, she has focused on developing private and exclusive brands to deliver fashion that can only be found at Walmart. At the close of 2019, Walmart had more than 600 fashion brands, including 150 premium exclusive brands. It has also partnered with celebrities Ellen DeGeneres and Sofia Vergara to develop two brands that started as online-only products and in 2018 began moving into stores.

Trying to Meet Fair Value in Experiential

As Walmart builds up strength in the Frictionless and Product Brand quadrants, it has also started to pay attention to changes on the experiential side of retailing.

Although Walmart is making significant strides as a global omnichannel retailer, it is still not the place consumers flock to for the most innovative shopping experiences. But as McMillon revamps stores to cater more to online/offline integration, he is also turning his eye toward becoming more relevant in the new world of social commerce. McMillon's goal is to add more "cool factor" and appeal for wealthier consumers.

One indication of progress on this strategy is the announcement that Walmart was making a joint bid, first with Microsoft and then with Oracle, to purchase a stake in the US operation of TikTok. The machinations showed Walmart was aware of the importance of social commerce (discussed more in chapter 7) and the importance of appealing to a younger shopper.

Although Walmart is by far the largest retailer with a leadership strategy to offer low prices, other retailers are competing fairly aggressively. Next, I will briefly describe some of their strategies.

Other Successful Low-Price Retailers

Dollar Stores

Even as other retailers suffer in the Amazon era, dollar stores have remained strong. Dollar General is aggressively opening new stores and reporting strong profits. Similarly, its rival Dollar Tree, which owns the Family Dollar chain, is also reporting growth.

Dollar stores are smaller in footprint than mass discounters or supermarkets. They target lower-income shoppers and focus on markets that are not necessarily well served by other retail giants. Dollar General, for example, is looking to open stores in rural and exurban locations that are located miles away from the nearest Walmart or other major retailers.

While in the past their merchandising has been somewhat of a mash-up, these stores have tightened up product assortments and focused more on groceries, household goods, and other consumables. While other retailers look to digital, these retailers are building new stores, as brick and mortar is central to their strategies.

Dollar stores are also benefiting indirectly from the Amazon effect. Currently, only about 70% of dollar-store customers have smartphones, which means the demographic of a typical dollar store shopper doesn't have significant overlap with online shoppers. Further, many of the transactions in a dollar store are made in cash, which is not possible in online shopping.

Evidence also shows that millennials who earn more than $100,000 are shopping at dollar stores. One study shows that about 29% of the millennial dollar-store customers earn over $100,000 annually—and account for about 25% of sales at those stores.[35]

Target

Target is another important retailer competing in the Low Price quadrant and is a direct competitor to Walmart. Like Walmart, Target has historically depended on big-box stores to drive revenues. But given the changing shopping environment, it has been growing its online business. Digital sales growth was 29% in 2019. Its online business was further boosted during the pandemic, growing by 141% during Q1 of 2020.[36]

Like Walmart, Target is building an omnichannel strategy, encouraging customers to order online and pick up in stores. Plans are in place to add curbside service for pickup of online orders and to add Saturday delivery. Target is improving supply chain and logistics capabilities by modernizing its supply chain. It recently acquired technology and talent from same-day delivery startup Deliv, a company that specializes in "last mile" delivery.

Though Target had in years past capitalized on a relatively high "design" merchandising mystique within its price points, earning itself the name "Tar-zhay," it has more recently seen its reputation suffer as more of its customers have relied on Amazon's superior convenience.

Target is responding successfully to the Amazon threat by introducing new private brands, such as the children's focused clothing line Cat & Jack, which had a very fruitful first-year launch. It is also looking to launch 12 new brands in infant (Cloud Island), maternity (Isabel Maternity), women's (A New Day), men's (Goodfellow & Co.), home (Project 62), and women's athletic fashion (JoyLab). In addition, Target is investing in new, fresh merchandising that it changes monthly. While customers responded favorably initially, the pandemic shifted priorities. Designated an essential retailer, Target was forced to focus on grocery and omnichannel delivery. Apparel sales declined as much as 40% during Q2 2020.[37]

In recent years, Target has moved away from big-box stores and has prioritized its small-format stores, which are aimed at three types of markets: urban centers, suburban centers, and college campuses.

These stores have focused on merchandise specifically for these types of customers and are also serving as fulfillment centers for online orders.

Target has announced some partnerships with DNVBs (see chapter 4) to cater to millennial customers, although its strategy is very different from what Lore was doing with Walmart. Rather than making acquisitions, Target has partnered with the new brands, such as Casper and the men's grooming subscription service Harry's. This partnering strategy is consistent with Target's history. In the past, Target developed its fashion brand cachet by partnering with premium luxury brands and trendy designers such as Michael Graves, Missoni, Proenza Schouler, and Isaac Mizrahi, among others. Target has also announced a new strategic partnership with beauty retailer Ulta to offer "shop-in-shop" destinations located near Target's existing beauty sections.

Aldi

Aldi is a German grocery store chain that now competes in the United States and sells privately branded knockoffs of established American foods. Aldi was founded by the Albrecht brothers, who worked in their mother's German retail business. They introduced the name "Aldi" in 1961 as a shortened version of Albrecht Diskont (Albrecht Discount). Aldi focuses on the bargain hunter.

Unlike traditional grocery stores, Aldi has no counter service departments; everything is self-service and packaged. Customers bag their own groceries. Stores are small, and they don't carry everything a more traditional grocery store might. Shoppers must pay for carts by deposit and return them, which eliminates the need for staffing requirements. There is no advertising.

The only staff in Aldi stores are forklift operators, cashiers, and maybe a security agent. Aldi private brands are the only brands; the motive to purchase at this store is completely based on low prices. Store brands look like US national brands, but they are not. The purchase process is very simple—there are no pricing trade-offs, there are no coupons, there are no sales. Estimates suggest Aldi's assortments of goods retail for 17% to 21% less than Walmart's.

Aldi is so far a small player and accounts for only 1.5% of the US grocery market, but it was growing at 15% in 2017. Plans are in place to remodel older stores and to open 400 new locations. The company has signaled low prices will be its singular advantage; if rivals compete on price, Aldi will respond. Aldi is planning to become the third-largest US grocery chain by late 2022 and was scheduled to debut 70 stores by the end of 2020.[38] Aldi is also growing its ecommerce services and has announced the expansion of curbside grocery pickup to almost 600 stores nationwide.

Conclusion

Given the appeal of low-price strategies, the competition in this quadrant is fierce. Walmart is the quadrant's biggest player and has the most to lose, but it is aggressively fighting to preserve its position. As Amazon opens more physical stores, including its own grocery chain, and leverages its acquisition of Whole Foods, competition is likely to heat up even further. Other low-price retailers like the dollar stores, Aldi, and Target are also aggressively protecting their market shares.

Although low prices are appealing to large segments of customers, if these retailers do not respond to changing customers' expectations in the other quadrants, particularly in the Frictionless quadrant, they may eventually lose out to Amazon, which is making online shopping the norm and can ruthlessly match prices if it wants and offer far superior service and convenience.

Chapter 4

The Power of the Brand
The Direct-to-Consumer Model

In This Chapter: Kahn Retailing Success Strategy
- Key Leadership Strength: Product Branding
- Secondary Leadership Strength: Lower Prices
- Fair Value in Frictionless and Experiential

As Walmart and Amazon compete in the Frictionless and Low Price quadrants, there is opportunity to capitalize on their relative weaknesses in the Product Brand and Experiential quadrants.

People have been predicting the death of brands forever. In the recession of the early 1990s, magazine covers were full of such declarations. A few years later, as Amazon introduced ecommerce to the masses, the argument went that the internet and the ease with which people could compare prices would kill brands.

Amid the 2008 recession, pundits suggested that people could no longer afford premium-priced products and that this new price sensitivity would linger well after economic conditions improved. But over and over, brands have been surprisingly resilient. For example, according to BrandZ, the total value of the brands in its Top 100 listing has risen at twice the rate of the US GDP.[39]

In this chapter, I focus on a special kind of brand: direct-to-consumer (DTC), or product brands that sell directly to the end user and typically do not partner with other retailers. They also do not sell branded products other than their own (although, again, they can and do in special circumstances). In essence, the idea is that the product's and retailer's brand name are one and the same.

The brands that I focus on here have two characteristics that lead to market leadership. First, the brand itself must offer an emotionally compelling proposition; it must have a unique brand narrative that speaks passionately to a core customer segment. Typically, these are brand names that resonate high quality *and* high design.

Second, these brands reinforce that customer commitment by leveraging the advantage gained by eliminating the middleman to offer a much better price value proposition and much closer customer connection. The value-pricing proposition is communicated not as a component of the brand (e.g., how "Walmart" means low prices) but as a function of creativity in the distribution system. With respect to the Kahn Retailing Success Matrix, this means they are leaders in the Product Brand quadrant, and they leverage that advantage to be leaders in the Low Price quadrant as well. They offer premium products for a great price.

DTC Brands Exist in Physical Stores and Online

There are two groups of successful retailers that use the DTC strategy to compete. First are vertical retail pioneers that have built powerful brands by selling in physical stores. I will use as examples two retailers that are to date successfully competing against Amazon in apparel and grocery: Zara, a retailer that invented "fast fashion" and continues to delight its core segment, and Trader Joe's, a quirky grocery retailer that people "f*@%ing love," according to Colorado food writer Jenn Wohletz.[40] Both retailers have passionate followers, and both use the fact that they sell directly to the end user to offer amazing price advantages.

Second is a group of relatively new DTC brands that began as ecommerce retailers and have similarly cultivated a passionate group of followers. These retailers have been dubbed "digitally native vertical brands" (DNVBs) by Andy Dunn, founder of Bonobos. The examples I will talk about are Warby Parker, Bonobos, and

Casper—each of which has reportedly passed the $100 million mark in annual revenues.

Like other ecommerce brands, DNVBs start online and market directly to the end user. But DNVBs differ on the "brand" dimension. As a group, these brands are, as Dunn explains, "maniacally focused on the customer experience."[41] They capture every transaction and interaction and commit to understanding and delivering real value to the customer.

Because of this customer-brand focus, these companies' product gross margins are at least double those of straight ecommerce retailers, according to Dunn, and contribution margins can be four to five times higher. Although these brands start online, the stronger ones typically extend to brick-and-mortar stores, which are extensions of their online presence and similarly tightly controlled.

Plotting the DTC Strategy on the Kahn Retailing Success Matrix

Since these strategies depend on clearly differentiated branding advantages, each retailer has a unique story to tell, which I will discuss later. Even though there are individual differences, the strategies of all the DTC-brand retailers have commonalities that can be mapped on the Kahn Retailing Success Matrix (see figure 4.1).

The critical advantage for both the legacy group and DNVBs begins with their strong product brand equity. They both build on their direct-distribution strategy to become leaders in the Low Price quadrant. Then, they build on these two leadership advantages to become market leaders in the Experiential quadrant. The two groups of DTC-brand retailers differ significantly in two ways. First, the legacy DTC-brand retailers are playing catch-up in the Frictionless quadrant. They have been leaders in the physical retailing world, and they are slower to respond to the changing shopping patterns as a function of online shopping and mobile commerce. On the other hand, DNVBs started online and then moved to physical stores, so they are already strong in the Frictionless quadrant.

Figure 4.1. Plotting DTC Brands on the Kahn Retailing Success Matrix

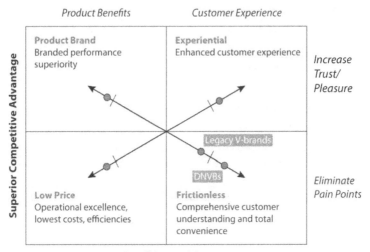

The second difference between the two groups is scale. While the DNVBs that I will discuss have passed the $100 million revenue mark, many newer startups have not yet met that mark, and most of these retailers are not yet profitable. On the other hand, the legacy retailers that I am discussing are significantly larger. For example, in 2019, Zara had estimated annual revenue of $20.6 billion and net profit of 2.7 billion euros. Similarly, Trader Joe's, which is a private company, reported $13.7 billion in revenues for 2019.

Superior Brand Performance

The critical leadership position of these DTC brands is that they offer strong brand equity that leads to long-term brand loyalty and community. These brands have established a compelling narrative and reinforce it through clever marketing and public relations strategies. Their reputations are cemented through strong customer-created word of mouth and viral videos. This means they are far above fair value in the Product Brand quadrant.

These brands usually do not advertise, but rather their message is delivered through user-generated content. This method of promotion not only is cost-effective but also builds trust and increases conversion through the principle of homophily—the tendency of people to have ties with people who are similar to themselves. In other words, if someone just like you recommends something, you are more likely to like it.

By controlling the entire distribution process, DTC brands can significantly improve the shopping experience both by removing pain points (as a result of having extensive customer data and continual customer interaction and feedback) and by providing personalized and fun experiential events and processes.

Lower Prices by Passing on Lower Costs Obtained by Eliminating Layers

There are several advantages to the direct model. First, through direct supply sources, retailers can achieve an average reduction of between 2% and 4% in cost of goods sold by eliminating inefficiencies in the supply chain. The direct relationship with suppliers also allows for speedy iterations on product design and more rapid response to demand changes and fashion trends.

Second, by eliminating other retailing layers in the distribution chain, DTC brands can eliminate excessive margins and pass on those savings. This allows them to compete more effectively on price. It also allows better control of brand narrative because no other retailer is communicating at the point of sale. Finally, it gives total control of customer data.

The other advantage of the direct model is better control of inventory, which helps manage the need for end-of-season price discounting. Typically, retailers using this strategy offer best price values using EDLP strategies and minimal to no price promotions. Thus, these brands are above fair value in the Low Price quadrant.

Exceptional Customer Experiences Within Physical Stores

The two types of DTC-brand retailers differ in their experiential strategies, but they both are way above fair value in offering physical-store experiences that excite their customers.

The legacy retailers, such as Zara, Trader Joe's, and Ikea, have always differentiated through their stores. Because these retailers are direct, they are closer to their customers and they can more quickly respond to customer needs in stores. As I will describe, for example, Zara's strategy is to listen intently to what customers want and to make sure those designs are in their stores as quickly as possible. Designs that don't sell are just as quickly eliminated. Trader Joe's stores, meanwhile, are unique, friendly, quirky, and again very responsive to customer tastes.

For DNVBs, the opening of their first physical stores allows for experimentation. Many of the first stores for these retailers were pop-ups, where consumer behavior could be observed before making costly investments. Also, because of extensive data from the online shopping experience, DNVBs benefit from intimate knowledge of how consumers browse, search, and shop. As a result, when DNVB retailers open their first stores, they look different from legacy retailers.

For many DNVBs, physical stores do not carry extensive inventory, but rather operate as showrooms that augment the digital experience rather than replace it. These showrooms provide opportunities for the consumer to touch and feel the product, interact with knowledgeable sales associates, and then make the final purchase online with at-home delivery.

Also, these new DNVB stores can offer experiential opportunities based on observed online behaviors. For example, Alo Yoga ("Alo" is an acronym for air, land, and ocean), which sells athletic apparel, opened a flagship store in Beverly Hills that houses yoga and fitness studios and has a lounge area for customers to relax. When Birchbox opened its first store in New York City, it organized it by product category rather than by brand. It also provides try-on bars and areas for the customer to learn.

Although they come from different directions, both types of retailers are able to hold their own on changing customer expectations with respect to in-store experiences, so both are above fair value in the Experiential quadrant.

Frictionless Convenience

The biggest difference between the two types of DTC brands is in the Frictionless quadrant. Since DNVBs started online, they can anticipate customer needs and respond similarly to the way Amazon responds to customer needs. Further, when they build physical stores, the online and offline experiences are instantly merged, as their customers are used to engaging with them one-on-one online. Like Amazon, DNVBs have extensive customer data and can design customer-centric strategies.

The legacy players are playing catch-up in this space. Some of them are rapidly developing omnichannel strategies that offer a seamless experience online and offline. Others are lagging, and their ecommerce presence is quite limited.

These strategies are plotted on the Kahn Retailing Success Matrix in figure 4.1.

Will These Retailers Be Successful?

When plotted on the matrix, these firms' strategies look quite strong. DNVB retailers are above fair value and are market leaders in all *four* quadrants (not just the suggested two), and the legacy retailers are above fair value in three of the four. These are obviously very compelling positions. But there are risks going forward.

Success of Legacy DTC Brands

For the legacy retailers, their weakness in the Frictionless quadrant can be an Achilles' heel. As Amazon gets stronger and stronger, customers' expectations in this quadrant will grow quickly, and customers will likely have little patience for retailers that cannot meet their convenience and delivery requirements.

Although Amazon is currently behind these retailers in terms of product brand and physical-store experiential environments, Amazon may seek to mitigate its weakness with strategic acquisitions. As noted in chapter 2, Amazon has made moves in fashion and grocery. Walmart is also aggressively pursuing a comprehensive omnichannel strategy and will be a force to reckon with globally.

Success of DNVB Retailers

DNVB retailers certainly have a viable strategy in place, and, so far, the math works. But these players are still quite small, and most are not profitable yet. If they can successfully scale up, they may be able to secure 30% operating margins (according to Lore), which would be viable. But they have to get over the hump—which some experts estimate at the $100 million to $200 million revenue mark.

The more successful DNVBs (such as Warby and Casper) have a fighting chance, but many of the smaller ones may get stuck in the $50 million revenue range. Alternatively, some may be bought out by retailers with deep pockets, such as when Walmart bought Bonobos and ModCloth, Unilever bought Dollar Shave Club, and Amazon bought Zappos. The "Top 25 DNVBs of 2017" sidebar lists the most successful DNVBs of that year.

Further, because these DNVBs have outside funding, they do not initially have to depend on cash flow and profitability to stay viable, as legacy brands did. This outside funding has helped DNVBs grow revenues much more quickly than legacy brands such as Nike, Patagonia, or Victoria's Secret. But eventually, DNVBs will still need two to three times their acquisition costs in margin to succeed.

Even if they can grow their revenues, the other problem with many of these new DNVBs is that they are often fashion brands. Many of them are banking on the tastes of millennials and Generation Z, and those tastes can be fickle. As retail commentator Richie Siegel suggested on the Business of Fashion website, "If Ralph Lauren is not

Top 25 DNVBs of 2017

- Alo Yoga
- Away Travel
- Birchbox
- Bonobos
- Casper
- Draper James
- Eloquii
- Everlane
- Glossier
- Harry's
- Kopari
- M.Gemi
- MM.LaFleur
- Morphe
- MVMT
- Outdoor Voices
- Parachute
- Perverse
- Quay Australia
- Rockets of Awesome
- Rothy's
- Saxx Underwear Co.
- Stance
- Thirdlove
- Warby Parker

Source: Pixlee, *The Top 25 Digitally Native Vertical Brands Report*, 2017, https://www.pixlee.com/download/the-top-digitally-native -brands-report-for-2017.

successful is it because of its model, or because the aesthetic has ceased to make sense to Gen Z'ers who shun grandpa's ties and blazers?"

How Did These Retailers Build Their Brand Narratives? Some Examples

The key to each DTC-brand retailer's success is its story, and each is unique. I will explore the marketing strategies of a few of the key retailers.

Zara

Zara, an international clothing retailer owned by Inditex and head-quartered in Spain, was founded in 1975. From the start, its mission has been to provide clothing that offers fashionable new designs (many times copies of popular, higher-priced fashion styles) made from quality materials—and that is affordable. To deliver, the company invested in a manufacturing and distribution process that could reduce lead times and react to trends more quickly. It invested in IT extensively and expanded globally. There are now over 7,000 Zara stores, and the retailer is still growing rapidly.

Zara was one of the originators of "fast fashion." Unlike the 12-to-18-month lead times of many of its fashion competitors, Zara could design and sell its collection in only four weeks. Most fashion brands are top-down, depending on well-known, talented designers to dictate the styles and fashions for the season. Zara works from the bottom up. The retailer watches trends and consumers' reactions to them, sees what people are wearing, monitors fashion blogs and fashion shows, and then produces designs that it believes will appeal to its customers.

This approach largely works well, although occasionally there are bumps in the road, primarily around accusations of putative plagiarism. The company has been sued by indie designers and high-end brands, but most of the cases have been resolved in Zara's favor because the company is able to tweak the design enough to get around copyright laws. This approach may not serve designers well, but customers react positively.

Being so customer focused means that Zara is less likely to guess wrong on which styles will be hot, and therefore less likely to have excess inventory at the end of the season. Zara also increases the desirability of its designs by producing less of each style and changing what it has on its sales floors frequently. This means that it carries much less inventory of any particular style, again lowering the risk of failed forecasting.

This frequent turnover of inventory drives the customer into the store more often to see what's new. It also teaches the customer that if she sees something she likes, she should purchase it right away because it might not be there next time. Zara's influence on the marketplace has been so great that traditional houses like Prada and Louis Vuitton have started to make four to six collections each year rather than just two.

With these strategies in place, each of the styles stays in the store for only three to four weeks, thus inventory turns 17 times per year. In order to stimulate more purchasing, Zara's founder, Amancio Ortega, has encouraged his customers to think of clothing as a perishable commodity, or as "disposable." People should buy the latest trends, wear them, then throw them out and buy the next trend.

The focus on "disposable clothing" has recently come under fire for imposing high environmental and social costs, forcing Zara to pivot to more sustainable strategies. Inditex (parent brand of Zara) CEO Pablo Isla said that by 2025, all of its brands will use sustainable or recycled materials and that renewable sources will power 80% of the energy consumed by its distribution centers, offices, and stores.[42] Its plan will allow it to source materials that have a better environmental profile, but still stay consistent with its overall value proposition to the consumer.

Critical to Zara's brand equity is that it can forecast and produce the hottest fashion designs reliably. That it has accomplished this consistently in a notoriously fickle industry is a function of the systems and processes that are in place. It is not a function of luck, but rather of Zara being very customer focused.

Importance of Physical Stores and Sales Associates

Central to its fashion strategy are sales associates who are trained to listen to customers and to report back what they hear. First thing every morning, floor staff and store managers meet to discuss the previous day's best-selling items, which items were returned, what shoppers said, and what trends they noticed on the floor. No detail is too small, and all customer comments are taken seriously.

These data points are entered into a system, and headquarters uses sophisticated technology to data-mine daily updates and use them to help determine future offerings. The data are used by in-house designers to make consumer-friendly, trend-appropriate offerings. In addition to the floor staff observing behavior in Zara stores, buyers visit universities, nightclubs, and other locales to see what people are wearing. Recently, they have also started monitoring social media, online talk, and bloggers.

Its marketing strategy is not based on advertising but rather on word of mouth and retail displays, so stores are a key part of its marketing. Zara's store priority is now focused on flagship stores in very high-traffic locations, frequently next to luxury brands such as Prada and Chanel. It is closing smaller stores. The store window displays showcase the most fashionable pieces in the collection and change often.

Zara's Vertically Integrated Supply Chain

Complementing this customer-centric approach is a vertically integrated supply chain that ships new products to stores twice a week. Better inventory control eliminates the need for warehouses.

Zara also has a sophisticated procurement and manufacturing approach. The more fashionable (and hence riskier) items are made in company-owned factories in Spain, northern Portugal, and Turkey. The items with more predictable demand patterns, such as basic T-shirts, are made with low-cost suppliers elsewhere. From its own factories in Spain, Zara transports its product by air directly to stores around the world, eliminating layers and making delivery times much faster than retailers that manufacture their goods in Asia can accomplish. This helps ensure that Zara is first with trendy fashions and has proved to be much more flexible.

Zara's Ecommerce Strategy

Although historically Zara's strength was in physical stores, it has recognized the changing environment and the trend toward more digital commerce. In 2020, Zara announced that it was closing 1,200 of its smaller stores and accelerating its digital transformation. The existing larger stores will be fitted with the latest sales integration technology, which will help facilitate omnichannel integration. As with other retailers, the closing of physical stores during the pandemic helped accelerate growth to the digital channel. Online sales rose as much as 50% during 2020, and Zara is now predicting that online sales will account for more than 25% of total sales (up from only 5.5% in 2017).[43]

With the new technology in place, customers will be able to pick up and return online purchases in-store. The stores will also each act as a fashion distribution hub, and the stores can fulfill ecommerce orders from their stockrooms, which are fully integrated with the online platforms.

Trader Joe's

Trader Joe's, which is owned by Aldi, has said its mission is to deliver high-quality food and beverage with a sense of warmth, friendliness, fun, individual pride, and company spirit. Like other retailers described in this chapter, Trader Joe's eliminates layers so it can get cost advantages and pass those along to end users. It buys direct from suppliers in volume, which results in better prices for goods. It does not charge suppliers slotting fees for putting items on the shelf, which further lowers the selling price.

Although Trader Joe's does sell third-party goods, experts estimate that 80% of Trader Joe's products are "in-house" and not available anywhere else. The retailer's website states: "We buy products we think are winners and that'll find a following among our customers. Sometimes it's a product we intend to stock as long as it sells well; and sometimes we buy a product which is in limited supply, sell through it, and you won't find it again. It's all part of the shopping adventure at Trader Joe's." So, like Zara, Trader Joe's encourages customers to buy when they see things and to understand that certain products may not always be available.

Trader Joe's has a vibe and is one of the few non-mega grocers that is succeeding in a retailing world of behemoths: Walmart, Amazon, Costco, and Target. No other chain offers what it does: unique, natural brands you can't get anywhere else. The Trader Joe's shopping experience continues to please customers who will often wait in long lines and deal with stock-outs without complaining, mostly due to their fierce loyalty to the quirky environment.

Trader Joe's Vulnerability

With Amazon's purchase of Whole Foods, Trader Joe's is certainly in the crosshairs. After the acquisition, when Amazon cut prices at Whole Foods, 10% of all Trader Joe's customers defected to Whole Foods. That figure went down to 6% in subsequent weeks, suggesting strong loyalty to Trader Joe's.

Trader Joe's also lags significantly in the Frictionless quadrant. Trader Joe's does not have a notable online strategy. You can order Trader Joe's groceries online, but they are delivered through third-party services. You can also order via Amazon.

Even during the pandemic, when many consumers started buying groceries online, the company announced that it did not have any plans to start an online service. Company officials said that although their customers were asking for online service, creating an online shopping system for curbside pickup or for delivery was too large an infrastructure undertaking. They are banking on "back to normal" behavior after COVID-19. While there were some blips in the early days of the pandemic with regard to protection of employees and stock-outs, Trader Joe's continued to receive rave reviews from its loyal customers.

Warby Parker

Warby Parker is often cited as the prototypical DNVB. The company was founded in 2010 in Philadelphia, when founders Neil Blumenthal, Dave Gilboa, Jeff Raider, and Andy Hunt were MBA students at Wharton.

The designer eyewear industry was a large market at the time, with over $65 billion of revenue, and was dominated by a single company, Luxottica, which had significant market share. This dominance was somewhat masked because the company operated under many different brand names. For example, Luxottica owns eyewear-only brands such as Ray-Ban, Oakley, and Oliver Peoples; it has the licenses for fashion brands such as Chanel, Versace, Polo, and D&G; it owns eyewear retailers, including LensCrafters, Sunglass Hut, and

Pearle Vision; and it works with Target and Sears in their optical divisions. It also owns the vision insurance company EyeMed.

Because of Luxottica's dominance, the industry had very high markups. Products whose manufacturing and distribution costs came in at $25 could be sold at $400 retail after including wholesale, licensing, and retail markups. Further, these products were sold almost exclusively in physical stores.

But the Warby Parker founders speculated that if they could persuade consumers to buy online and if they could manage their entire distribution cycle by selling directly to end users (thus eliminating many layers), they could produce a high-quality product at a quarter of the retail price.

Customer-centric Innovations That Built the Brand

How could consumers be persuaded to purchase eyeglasses online without trying them on?

Warby Parker's first big innovation to solve this problem was its Home Try-On program, in which consumers could try up to five frames at home for free for five days. This program was incredibly successful right out of the gate. It was convenient, was easy, eliminated risk, and offered people high-quality glasses at an amazing price: $99. Equivalent designer prescription glasses were going for $300 and more at the time.

There were other, unanticipated benefits of the Home Try-On program. It turns out that people are pretty bad at determining for themselves which glasses fit their faces. So, when people received their glasses at home, they would frequently post photos of themselves on social media sporting different frames and asking friends for advice. This generated trusted public awareness of the brand. More than 50% of sales were generated through word-of-mouth referrals.

True to the DNVB mantra, the Warby founders were maniacally focused on customer service. They made their website user friendly, anticipating and answering any questions that a consumer would want to ask a sales associate in a physical store. Sometimes, consumers emailed questions and the founders themselves replied. All this attention to detail paid off: Warby's net promoter score was over 85, higher than those of Apple and Amazon.

In addition to the powerful word-of-mouth referrals, Warby had a good story to tell, and the media were interested. One of the first publications that wrote about Warby was *GQ*, which called it "the Netflix of eyewear." Warby hit its first-year sales target in three weeks and generated a wait list of 20,000 people. Soon, other fashion magazines and more mainstream media were telling the company's story as well.

Warby continued to innovate with clever marketing and retailing strategies. For example, during New York Fashion Week, Warby had friends and some professional models go to the New York Public Library the day before the Fashion Week events formally started. Warby then invited reporters to go to the library, and since it was a slow day, many reporters were available.

At a set time, each of the Warby representatives, who were scattered throughout the library sitting at different tables, held up a book covered with the Warby brand's light-blue color. Each book had written on it a title, which was the name of one of the company's eyeglass styles. (Warby's eyeglass style names are all famous literary references.) Having everyone hold up these light-blue books at the same time resulted in vivid visual imagery.

The coordinated action made for great photographs, and the event was covered widely. Over time Warby created other provocative events and put together pop-up stores with interesting themes. It retrofitted a school bus as an eyeglass store and drove around the country in this "bus-store" visiting campuses. All the activity generated widespread media coverage in the *New York Times*, *Vogue*, *Esquire*, *WWD*, *Forbes*, *People*, the *Wall Street Journal*, and *Glamour*.

Adding to this compelling brand narrative was exceptional customer service fueled by engaged employees. The people who worked at Warby were also fervent believers in the brand—especially because Warby promised to donate one pair of eyeglasses to someone in need for every pair it sold. Employees became loyal ambassadors of the brand.

Warby personifies everything a successful DNVB should be: an efficient distribution channel delivering a high-quality product at a reasonable price directly to the consumer. It has a valuable brand narrative and strong customer community that generates tons of social media and word of mouth to promote the brand.

Warby was also one of the first DNVBs to consider opening stores. Based on information gathered from pop-up stores and bus trips, it opened its first physical showroom in New York City. Analyzing data carefully after that opening, it learned that physical stores did not cannibalize online sales, but rather increased sales overall. Opening physical stores in the right locations with an eye for whimsy, design, and attention to the local area became a priority. It now has over 60 stores in the United States and continues to grow.

Warby is definitely a success story. It has raised $215 million and has been valued at $1.2 billion. Its latest move is to fund a $15 million optical lab in upstate New York that will help with greater quality control and faster delivery. It is also exploring ways to assess visual prescriptions via digital applications on a personal device.

Bonobos

Bonobos was launched in 2007 by Andy Dunn and Brian Spaly as an exclusively online retailer with the goal of selling men's pants that promised a great fit and style while minimizing time and hassle. Their product—with a curved waistband, a medium rise, and a tailored thigh fit designed to eliminate the "khaki diaper butt"—was much better than alternatives and soon inspired word of mouth. The brand grew.

Bonobos expanded to include men's shirts, sweaters, and jackets. In 2012, Dunn (Spaly left in 2009 to run Trunk Club), recognizing the need for customers to "touch and feel" in the apparel category (especially clothing that is marketed on fit), set up an exclusive partnership with Nordstrom to sell Bonobos product in its 100 Nordstrom stores. This was a win-win for both partners. For Bonobos, it was helpful to get scale. For Nordstrom, the DNVB brought a younger customer into the store. Nordstrom also saw it as an opportunity to improve its own digital practices.

Eventually, Bonobos opened its own physical stores, called "guideshops." These stores were unlike normal men's retailing stores in that they were showrooms only—they had no inventory. Given that they didn't have to carry full inventory, the showrooms could keep items for every size and style so the customer could try anything on in the store and never have to experience stock-outs. After trying on the product, the customer could order online and have the product delivered at home. The stores turned out to be the best customer acquisition channel for Bonobos.

Casper

Casper was founded in 2013 and launched in 2014. Like the Warby founders, Casper's creators recognized the mattress industry as a large market (an over $14 billion business) dominated by two major companies: Tempur Sealy and Serta Simmons, which together controlled over 70% of bedding wholesale shipments. The industry was growing, but primarily by raising prices.

Consumer Reports reported that mattresses carried a heavy price tag because the margins in the category were higher than any other product in a furniture store. Frequently gross profit margins were 30% to 40% for wholesalers and retailers.[44] High-end luxury models could command even higher margins.

And the sales process was often so unpleasant that people couldn't wait to get out of the store. Most customers knew nothing about mattresses and were embarrassed to lie on a mattress and imagine sleeping to test it (especially with people watching). Delivery was also slow.

As Warby did with its Home Try-On program, Casper came up with a clever innovation that made the process easier and generated great social media and viral word-of-mouth publicity. It figured out how to deliver a mattress in a box (the size of a mini fridge) on a bicycle. Customers would video themselves opening up the boxes and post the videos on Instagram. Casper also promised a risk-free experience: People could try the product for 100 nights, and if they didn't like it, Casper would pick up the mattress and take it back.

Casper also took the pain out of the decision-making process by limiting choice. It offered only one type of mattress, designed as a combination of memory and latex foam. Casper priced its mattress well below prices of the other mattresses on the market.

Although other online-centric mattress startups exist, including Leesa, Yogabed, and Tuft & Needle, Casper is probably the most famous. The Casper model was so successful that it generated revenues of over $100 million in less than two years. Its brand promise? To provide the best mattress possible at an affordable price, sell a single model, and deliver it quickly for free—with a 100-day trial period.

Like other DNVBs, Casper has recently opened physical stores. Casper operates around 60 stores and has plans to partner with world-class retailers like Costco, Target, and Sam's Club to help distribute its product.[45]

Other Retailers That Have Learned from the DNVB Playbook

DNVBs have inspired other retailers to experiment with showrooms that do not stock inventory but offer retailers a way to interact with their customers, build relationships, and collect useful data for future proactive activity and recommendations. For example, Samsung opened a store in New York City where customers can play with the company's newest devices and gadgets, learn how to use smart appliances, and experiment with VR.

There is no pressure to buy—in fact, the only things that can be purchased in the store are coffee and bagels. Samsung hopes it instead builds customer knowledge and loyalty for the brand. The store also offers events that draw in customers—the first year included a performance by Gwen Stefani, cooking demonstrations, and more. The company estimated that within the first 10 months of opening, more than a half-million people visited the space.

Nordstrom has also expressed interest in trying out the showroom idea. The first Nordstrom Local prototype launched in West Hollywood in 2017. This store features nail beauty services, tailoring, and style advice. In the same vein as Bonobos's guideshops, it doesn't have inventory but rather allows customers to check out and try on garments, then go online to order. The new store has dressing rooms and a bar. Nordstrom Style Boards provide personalized fashion recommendations that can be viewed on a smartphone, and items can then be purchased directly from Nordstrom.com. Although there is no buyable inventory, personal stylists can order the items, which can be picked up that same day at the store if the order is made before 2 p.m.

Conclusion

Many retailers that are successfully holding their own in this disruptive retailing environment are engaging in DTC strategies. These retailers sell their branded product brands directly to the end user. The successful ones have a compelling brand proposition and have leveraged significant cost advantages from eliminating layers both in distribution and in the supply chain. They have passed these cost advantages on to their customers and are able to sell high-quality, premium-branded products at low prices.

There are two classes of DTC brands. The first is the legacy brands that built this strategy through their physical stores. According to a 2019 Interbrand survey, some of the most valuable brands in the world fit this model: H&M, Zara, and Ikea, all of which rank in the top 30 globally.[46] These brands are doing well even with the threat of Amazon's entry into their business. They have private brands that cannot be purchased anywhere else, and they have very loyal customers. As the shopping experience shifts more to online purchasing, the challenge for these brands is to keep their dominance in the new channel and to make sure that they offer an integrated online-offline experience. (These brands did take a hit in 2020, when nonessential retailing was handicapped, but all three are still in the top 40.)[47]

The other DTC brands, the DNVBs, started online and have since moved into physical stores. These brands have passionate, loyal communities that help promote the brands through active social media engagement. Because they started in the digital world, they have amassed a great deal of data about their customers and can offer high-quality products at a low price and provide exceptional online and offline customer experiences. Their challenge now is to scale up. The most successful of these new breeds—Warby Parker, Casper, and Bonobos—have passed the $100 million revenue mark but are still much smaller than the traditional retailers. Many of them are also depending on external funding rather than cash flow and profitability to fund their businesses.

Chapter 5

The Paradox of Luxury
When Low Prices and Accessibility Are Undesirable

In This Chapter: Kahn Retailing Success Strategy
- Key Leadership Strength: Unparalleled Luxurious Product and Brand Superiority
- Secondary Leadership Strength: Luxurious Customer Experience
- Fair Value in Frictionless Becoming More Important
- Luxury Brands Refrain from Lower-Price Strategies and Halt Counterfeiting

In spite of continued calls for price transparency and the unique catastrophic effects of the COVID-19 pandemic on the luxury industry, with some analyses suggesting as much as 30% to 40% contraction in 2020, the luxury industry will survive. For over 100 years, the desirability of exclusivity, prestige, and status signaling provided by luxury brands has resulted in strong growth. Historically, the luxury retail market has grown faster than other categories, even following economic downturns. Evidence shows that once again younger populations, including millennials and Gen Z, are starting to connect with luxury brands, just like their baby boomer and Generation X parents.

What Is Luxury? And How Does It Differ from Premium Priced?

Luxury brands are more expensive than premium-priced brands, but there are other important differences. Premium-priced brands are defined by a quality-to-price value ratio, in which higher quality will demand a higher price. But for luxury, higher quality is necessary but not sufficient. Adam Smith defined luxury brands as not only very expensive but also limited in supply and difficult to procure.

Luxurious products and experiences are defined by unique characteristics that cannot be copied, like heritage, legacy, tradition, blood (family), celebrity, and, more recently, designers. True luxury brands are timeless icons, magical, and more like religion and art than commerce. Just as it is difficult to put a quality/price value on a Monet painting, so luxury brands have a heritage that is irreproducible. "Luxury brands are the ambassadors of local culture and refined art de vivre," wrote Jean-Noël Kapferer, a European expert on luxury.[48]

Historically, true luxury represents the antithesis of a customer-centric focus. Rather, luxury heritage and celebrated designers are the arbiters of taste and design, reinforcing the idea that luxury is aspirational. Luxury revels in beliefs about scarcity. Items that are hard to get, maybe even restricted or requiring approval to purchase (e.g., the long waiting lists for Birkin handbags), are made even more valuable.

Luxury mandates noncomparisons, mitigating price competition and price/quality trade-offs. For example, champagne comes from France's Champagne district, or it is not champagne. Similarly, cognac is defined on an ambiguous scale—not by exact age, which is an alignable attribute, but rather by XO (extra old) or VSOP (very superior old pale).

Luxury Brands Control Distribution and Pricing

Total control of the manufacturing and distribution chain is a requirement for the most exclusive luxury brands. Hermès, probably the most prestigious, controls everything under its brand name and does not issue licenses. Although luxury brands may be sold at luxury retailers such as Saks, Neiman Marcus, Le Bon Marché, Galeries Lafayette, Harrods, or Selfridges, many of the luxury brands prefer to go direct to exercise more control. All of these measures limit accessibility.

True luxury brands also do not generally discount, even if they have excess inventory. Because of the short shelf life of seasonal brands, at these top luxury houses seasonal products are priced 20 to 30 times higher than the more timeless designs, and only a limited amount is produced. If these seasonal products do not sell in time for the next inventory shift, they may be burned rather than discounted (although this practice has generally been discontinued due to bad publicity).

These hallmarks of luxury suggest a different mandate for growth. Traditional growth by increasing market share, frequently through lowering price and increasing distribution channels, goes against the rules of luxury. This is the "paradox of luxury." If everyone can afford or obtain luxury, the aspirational aspect is destroyed.

Many luxury brands have been stung by brand erosion when they have succumbed to the short-term lure of issuing licenses and expanding distribution. The luxury landscape is replete with examples of brands like Pierre Cardin, Ralph Lauren, or Coach, which all had to work hard to regain their past glory after overreaching to increase short-term revenues.

Growth for luxury has to come from careful strategies that build on luxury strengths of exclusivity and price premiums. There are two paths to growth that preserve the strengths of luxury: (1) building relationships with key affluent customers over time and (2) building a diversified brand portfolio, which plays to their leadership strength on the Kahn matrix.

Growth Strategies for Luxury: The Importance of Customer Relationships

Since the very high-end luxury market is quite small, the best avenue for growth is through building long-term relationships with these customers. Traditionally, these relationships have been built through dedicated, personal face-to-face interactions generated through the physical luxury channel. However, with growing expectation that personalized and customized service has to be delivered 24/7 wherever the customer is, luxury is now beginning to depend on technology to nurture relationships.

Most luxury profits come from a small percentage of shoppers. For Mytheresa, an online luxury shopping business that was acquired by Neiman Marcus Group, a few VIP clients accounted for about 30% of sales.[49] At Moda Operandi, top clients account for almost 50% of sales. At Neiman Marcus, 3% of its top customers who spend at least $10,000 per year drive 40% of its sales, with a retention rate of 97%.

A growth strategy that builds on luxury brand advantages should leverage these top customers and build a strong relationship over time. According to Neiman Marcus Group CEO Geoffroy van Raemdonck, the best customers have three characteristics that make them especially valuable and worth prioritizing. First, profitability comes from high-quality customers, those who have the highest customer lifetime value. Second, the best customers are loyal not only to a retailer but also to their own sales associates. Luxury is about personal service and building personal relationships that instill loyalty and guarantee a high retention rate. Finally, in today's world, the best customers are also digitally connected.[50]

The relationship typically starts in a physical store, where a sales associate begins to build a trust relationship with a customer. Luxury brands and retailers offer these top customers VIP service involving fancy dinners, travel, and exclusive intimate designer showings. Amid the pandemic, these one-on-one relationships were mimicked online through digital Zoom cocktail and wine tastings and celebrity online workout classes. Physical products, food, alcohol, and flowers were shipped in advance. Aside from these physical experiences, the store remains important because it allows for alterations and a place to touch and feel the product. During the pandemic, the store facilitated curbside pickups, in-store private appointments, and in some cases, home visits.

But the avenue for growth is through digital, which allows retailers to scale at very low cost and provides data to assess customer preferences and to allow for customized recommendations. At Neiman Marcus and other high-end retailers, a sales associate can typically leverage three channels: the physical store, the online shopping experience, and the sales associate's own app, which for Neiman is appropriately called Connect. Seamless integration across channels allows the sales associate to collect data—not only for each customer but for all customers in the elite set. This provides intelligence that is leveraged by AI and can help the sales associate determine when to call—and with what offer.

This personalization maximizes the likelihood of pleasing the customer with the perfect suggestion at the right time and place. The more data collected across the customers who indicate what they like or don't like, the smarter the interaction, and the better the recommendations. For multibrand retailers like Neiman, they can get insights from different brands and across different customers, which allows them to microtarget and not only provide recommendations based on past behavior but also offer surprises likely to delight.

Brands Move to Direct Relationships

The move to new technology interfaces has also accelerated some major luxury brands' moves toward DTC relationships, rather than depending on multibrand wholesale distributors. The advantage of DTC gives stronger luxury brands better control over pricing, brand experience, and inventory. With the exit of some of the bigger brands, luxury wholesalers/department stores have more open space to dedicate to new up-and-coming fashion and luxury brands.

For example, the Galeries Lafayette store in Paris on the Champs-Elysées started featuring new, younger brands such as Bode, Craig Green, and Telfar. The advantage is that these brands can inspire newness and innovation and attract younger consumers. Galeries Lafayette stores are looking to increase the share of smaller luxury labels from 30% to 40% over the next few years.[51] Another way to feature the new brands is through pop-up arrangements. London's Selfridges has introduced pop-up space to highlight new curations by up-and-coming designers.

The trade-offs between the direct brand relationships and the multibrand wholesalers are interesting. For the luxury brand, direct relationships make sure the customer is given an authentic experience. For brands, this is critical. The direct relationship also allows the brand to better control inventory and makes comparisons with others more difficult, thus ensuring tighter loyalty. Gucci, Louis Vuitton, and Chanel are all moving more toward vertically integrated strategies. On the other hand, multibrand wholesalers offer the high-end customer the advantage of choice. José Neves, CEO of Farfetch, believes there will always be demand for multibrand retailers.

Bringing in the New Generation

Experts predict that millennials and Gen Z will account for 45% of the luxury market by 2025. Will this idea of exclusivity and aspirational values jibe with the goals of the younger generation who purport to value transparency and authenticity?

Some studies have shown that the younger generations seem to value experiences more than material possessions, so at the very least luxury brands must provide not just superior product brands but also overall luxurious, exclusive customer experiences. Younger, digitally native generations value convenience and expect 24/7 environments. Luxury has to consider how to make its products and experiences more accessible without losing the exclusivity.

Early indications suggested Gen Z would take to luxury more than millennials. Millennials came of age during the Great Recession, whereas Gen Z arrived in flusher economic times. COVID-19, however, has cast some doubt on this generalization. Gen Z'ers, although mobile savvy, have not abandoned physical stores. Some of the more interesting retail concepts have capitalized on Gen Z's proclivity for social media and physical retail by providing settings where nothing is sold but customers can come to a well-designed interactive physical environment and take photos of themselves to be posted on Instagram or Facebook.

There are some marked differences between younger consumers and their parents. The first is that younger generations are not averse to sharing luxury products with others; they do not insist on primary ownership. This has helped both the rental market (e.g., Rent the Runway) and the pre-owned market (e.g., Real) to grow substantially. And the possibility of sharing affects not only the purchasing of goods that are not new, but also the consideration of a secondary market when making new purchases. That lessens initial price sensitivity, an objective consistent with the goals of luxury. Reusable luxury also helps eliminate wasted resources, a trend generally supportive of the bigger luxury brands. The most in-demand pre-owned brands are Chanel, Louis Vuitton, Gucci, Burberry, and Dior.

A second distinction is a sincere concern about sustainability and social responsibility. According to surveys, younger luxury consumers are more concerned with the environment and animal care, although all generations are concerned with ethical manufacturing. Luxury brands have reacted by raising the proportion of renewable raw materials in their products.

The future of luxury can be seen by what is happening in China. For example, Louis Vuitton collaborated with *League of Legends*, an online game created by Riot Games (which is a California-based developer but owned by Tencent) during its Legends World Championship. LV used the online game as a way to showcase its new collection, which was viewed by 99.6 million unique viewers worldwide.[52] Other luxury brands formed similar partnerships: Gucci partnered with Tencent focusing on KOL (key opinion leader) marketing, while Michael Kors launched a campaign on Douyin (the Chinese version of TikTok). Typically, younger consumers are less interested in brand heritage and more interested in brand interaction.

Plotting This Strategy for Luxury Brands on the Kahn Retailing Success Matrix

Historically, luxury retailers have competed by providing unequaled high-quality branded products, but leadership in one quadrant is not sufficient in today's very highly competitive retailing world. Most of the luxury retailers are seeking to leverage their brand cachet to produce superior luxurious customer experiences as well. The brand product strategy for luxury has to preserve exclusivity and prestige, which necessitates a specific brand portfolio concept (described below).

Luxury retailers also have to be mindful of ever-increasing customer expectations in the Frictionless quadrant and meet those expectations. Although initially resistant to digital commerce for fear of making luxury too convenient, many luxury retailers and brands have since found ways to use the digital interfaces that offer 24/7 accessibility as a means to build on their exclusive and personal relationships with their customers.

Finally, there is often pressure on luxury brands to offer price discounts, but lowering the price runs counter to the principles of luxury. Top luxury brands make a point of pricing exorbitantly high. This is the definition of the paradox of luxury: Higher prices frequently make the products more valuable by signaling exclusivity. For the typical expectation of a reasonable price, the price of luxury must be plotted as below common expectations. These ideas are plotted in figure 5.1.

In the next sections, I will outline the strategies that luxury retailers, accessible luxury retailers, and new ecommerce entrants are developing to compete in all four of the Kahn Retailing Success Matrix quadrants.

Primary Value: Unparalleled Luxurious Product Brand Superiority

Growth for luxury can come by developing deeper relationships with the best customers. But another option for growth is through a

Figure 5.1. Plotting Luxury on the Kahn Retailing Success Matrix

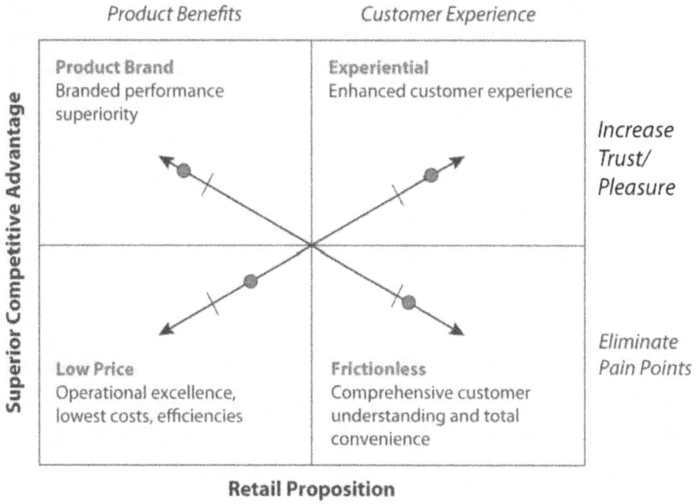

Product Benefits   *Customer Experience*

Product Brand
Branded performance
superiority

Experiential
Enhanced customer experience

*Increase
Trust/
Pleasure*

*Eliminate
Pain Points*

Low Price
Operational excellence,
lowest costs, efficiencies

Frictionless
Comprehensive customer
understanding and total
convenience

Superior Competitive Advantage

Retail Proposition

diversified brand strategy. Luxury brands typically can obtain large margins because of the intangibles that come along with the exclusive brand name. If retailers could leverage this brand identity across a range of product lines, that would offer both cost advantages for them and incentives for customers to trust new products. The trick is to stretch the brand name to include lower-priced items without diluting the top items. Luxury retailers have two goals for their branding strategy: build a brand that promotes luxury values, and leverage that brand without diluting it to grow the market. There are two basic ways that luxury retailers can accomplish these goals: the "branded house" strategy and the "house of brands" strategy.

Branded House Strategy

In the branded house strategy, all of the items in the product line are branded with one name. The growth opportunity comes from leveraging luxury brand products into lower-priced categories that offer more potential market share but risk diluting the luxury brand name. The branded house strategy is based on a portfolio pyramid model. The tip of the pyramid focuses on high-margin, high-priced couture, a small sliver of the overall market demand catering to the very rich. The bottom of the pyramid, which is large, represents a more price-restricted demographic. The bottom of the pyramid, because of the volume, can frequently generate more profit even at lower margins.

For example, Chanel sells haute couture gowns for tens of thousands of dollars, but also sells beauty products and fragrances for under $100.

Sometimes, the two markets in the pyramid are separated by channel: The high-end products are sold in flagship stores, while the lower-priced products are sold in outlets. The key is to make sure the lower-priced and prolific goods do not destroy the brand's elitism.

Another method within the branded house strategy is to have subbrands or endorsed brands differentiated from the couture brand but still benefiting from the brand halo. For example, Ralph Lauren has the Collection Label, which is higher priced than Polo and outlet brands. Within Armani, there is the higher-priced Giorgio Armani and the lower-priced Emporio Armani. There are also lower-price diffusion product lines that are, in essence, promoted as separate brand names but are endorsed by the luxury house, such as AX by Armani.

Another way luxury brands leverage brand equity is through the use of logos. Logos can be overdone, and the presence or absence of logos seems to go in and out of style. Generally, those using luxury to signal status prefer logos, but those who want to be considered elite (and not accessible to the masses) disdain logos. In cases of the latter, luxury "codes" let people in the know understand the value of the product without an ostentatious brand name that makes the appeal widespread. For Chanel, codes include the camellias, double Cs, pearls, tweed jacket, quilted bag, and two-toned shoe.

House of Brands Strategy

The house of brands is a portfolio of stand-alone brands that cater to different segments and price points. This way, one brand name does not contaminate or dilute another. European multinational luxury goods conglomerates like LVMH, Richemont, and Kering follow this strategy. LVMH owns Louis Vuitton, Céline, Dior, Fendi, Givenchy, Loro Piana, Marc Jacobs, and more. Kering owns Gucci, Bottega Veneta, Yves Saint Laurent, Alexander McQueen, and others. Maintaining and building multiple brands is costlier than investing in just one brand but mitigates risk. Also, with the house of brands strategy, growth can come through acquisition.

The two biggest luxury players, LVMH and Kering, have different philosophies. LVMH primarily depends on heritage brands, typified by its most popular brand, Louis Vuitton, originally a luggage maker. Kering is built more on fashion labels, like Yves Saint Laurent and Balenciaga. More recently, LVMH has developed a more diverse portfolio of brands in categories, while Kering has been successful by cultivating creative design talent.

Although not precisely similar to classic European royalty luxury, street and urban brands have some of the same characteristics. Supreme, launched in 1994, became the brand of choice for rebellious New York skaters and artists who were not only customers but also employees. The brand worked with famous designers, artists, musicians, and photographers who all contributed to its unique identity. The first store opened in New York followed by a limited number of stores around the world.

Accessible Luxury
Accessible luxury brands priced more affordably can be very profitable, because they can reach larger audiences. But this volume comes at the risk of longer-term brand dilution. Recently, many accessible luxury brands have been reexamining their brand strategies.

For example, Marc by Marc Jacobs was a diffusion brand that launched in 2001 and offered products priced under $500. It was profitable, but with economics that were less attractive than other European luxury brands, which could command higher price premiums and operate as vertical business models. In 2014, LVMH announced it would merge Marc and the main brand, Marc Jacobs, into one brand. Under this brand name, it offered contemporary and premium products, exercised tighter control over wholesale distribution, and reduced off-price sales and promotions. This discipline, while protecting the brand, resulted in a loss of revenue—almost 50% in three years.

Similar woes befell Coach, whose sales plummeted in 2014 as customers lost interest in its purses because of an overreliance on outlet sales and discounts. Victor Luis took over as CEO with a bold strategy to change the direction of the company. He purposely shrank the business and prioritized quality over mass-market quantity and discounting. He closed dozens of stores, ended online flash sales, and began to pull out of department stores. This strategy hurt top-line sales in the short term, with the goal of building long-term profitability and stability.

Luis adopted the European luxury style through the house of brands strategy, acquiring Kate Spade and Stuart Weitzman. He also changed the name of the company to Tapestry, with Coach becoming one of Tapestry's divisions. Michael Kors has followed a similar strategy of purchasing brands, and also renaming the holding company to Capri Holdings Limited. Michael Kors purchased Jimmy Choo, and while Tapestry has so far stuck to US brands, Michael Kors acquired the European brand Versace.

Tory Burch is one accessible luxury brand that, from the start, had limited off-price discounting and a tight control of outlet distribution. Hers is an American sportswear brand, which the company describes as classic yet modern, distinguished by a global and eclectic aesthetic. The brand launched in February 2004 as a full omnichannel model—both retail and ecommerce—which was very unusual at the time. Her brand support was always on social media; she did not wage classic advertising campaigns.

Burch's digital strategy included not only product descriptions but also articles, ideas, and other illustrations that supported her fashion. The story that unfolded on her social media was personal. The website reflects her personal history, starting with the life she lived growing up with her parents, Buddy and Reva Robinson (her most famous product, her ballet flats, is named after her mother), to her current life as a working mother.

Another unusual aspect of her business is the Tory Burch Foundation, which supports the economic empowerment of women entrepreneurs and their families. This adds up to an authentic, intimate brand different from others in this space. It builds loyalty not through price discounts but through an organic, resonating message.

Building a Luxury Customer Experience

As the retailing world becomes more competitive and younger consumers are more empowered, customers want more than a strong luxury brand product. Luxury retailers need to offer more, and most are investing in luxurious customer experiences to build on their legacies. The luxury stores are becoming destinations in and of themselves, going beyond shopping to become entertainment and dining destinations.

Continued Importance of Physical Stores

As more brands either start online or add ecommerce to their strategies, the online world of retail has become competitive. Many digital and luxury brands have turned to physical stores or pop-ups for customer acquisition. In January 2020, Matt Alexander, CEO of Neighborhood Goods, said on a panel at the National Retail Federation "Big Show" that "physical retail is more effective than a billboard" when it comes to customer acquisition.[53] This intuition is similar to what the DNVBs, like Warby Parker, discovered (detailed in chapter 4). The successful integration of strategically placed physical showrooms can increase, not cannibalize, online purchasing. Studies have shown that customers who visit a showroom are more likely to purchase more, spend more money, and return fewer products than customers who did not visit a showroom, controlling for other factors. Studies have also found that time between purchases fell, while consumers bought in more categories. Stores are also important for discovery; studies show discretionary spending remains highest in physical spaces.

Shopping as entertainment has also emerged as a trend. Luxury brands are forging closer relationships with hospitality. In the same way that people make reservations for restaurant experiences, they can now plan shopping excursions. The shopping experience has become the motivation, while the end purchase is the souvenir.

The pandemic has made safety an important part of the experience, particularly with regard to the "touch and feel" aspect. Some retailers are turning to augmented reality to provide a sanitary alternative. In addition to the makeup counter, AR is being used with apparel companies for virtual try-on experiences. Gucci has a partnership with Snapchat that allows users to try on shoes through an AR lens. Stores have also accelerated the development of contactless payment, preordering, and pickup curbside or at the airport.

The Place to Be

Apple stores have always understood the value of extraordinary retail experiences. Ron Johnson, who opened the first Apple retail store in 2001, created Genius Bars and friendly welcoming environments so customers could test Apple products. The stores were immediately successful and made more money per square foot than Tiffany & Co.

Apple stores have become town squares or community centers. They are "gathering places" where consumers can hang out and even take classes on coding, music, and photography. Apple's new strategy is to open fewer, larger stores to engage customers with everything that is Apple. The stores fulfill Steve Jobs's vision. He told his employees that with respect to their customers, "your job is not to sell; your job is to enrich their lives and always through the lens of education."[54]

The Drop Culture Experience

One way Supreme secured its loyal base was by capitalizing on the principle of scarcity and exclusivity in a different way. This brand was the originator of the "drop culture." Unlike other brands that introduce new products by season, Supreme releases 5 to 15 on a weekly basis.

Each week in which there is a drop, Supreme customers have to be at stores on Thursday at exactly 11 a.m.—and even if they are, they may not leave with the product. The brand delivers a certain number of items, deliberately limited so that not everyone gets one. Customers wait outside the store for hours before the specified drop time.

Products offered at the drops would sell out in minutes. Loyal customers who were lucky enough to get one would frequently share their bounty on social media. Even waiting in line had brand value; the line in some ways became the brand community, the brand experience. The *New York Times* called this the "cult of the line."[55] Traditional luxury brands noticed the success, resulting in a collaboration between Supreme and Louis Vuitton in 2017.

Luxury Pop-Ups

Luxury retailers are also using pop-ups as opportunities to create experiences. This is their own version of the drop, since they only exist for a limited amount of time. In 2017, Louis Vuitton opened a pop-up store on Madison Avenue in New York dedicated to the Louis Vuitton and Jeff Koons collaboration. The pop-up store covered 4,200 square feet and honored the original works of da Vinci, Van Gogh, Fragonard, and Rubens, with enlarged prints and descriptions of the work on free-standing angled panels. The pop-up offered exclusive leather goods and accessories that came from this collaboration.

Tiffany & Co., Louis Vuitton, and Chanel have invested in pop-up stores for the holiday season. Chanel opened a pop-up called Coco Club for a single day and dedicated it to the brand's Boy-Friend watch. In addition to product displays, it offered a makeup studio, café, and library. A numerologist was available to give guests personalized readings.

Controlling Pricing and Counterfeiting

The paradox in luxury retailing is that unlike in most other retail transactions, where lower prices are attractive, making the luxury product too affordable to purchase undermines the brand's value. Luxury pricing must be based on the perceived value to the customer, but this value does not rest solely on the quality or functional aspect of the product. It must also take into account the brand heritage or aspirational value. Similarly, luxury firms try to discourage any comparative framing in pricing. And unlike normal laws of supply and demand, in luxury pricing, increasing prices can actually increase demand.

This has not stopped other types of retailers from trying to fill that gap by providing discount options. Amazon, Alibaba, and JD .com all have third-party retailers flocking to their marketplace platforms and reselling branded goods at deep discounts or, worse still, selling unauthorized counterfeit products. Studies have estimated the loss from the counterfeiting of luxury goods or brands at over $10 billion in lost sales per year. Luxury brands have tried to crack down by buying back inventory from unauthorized sellers and working with big online players to control the activity. Luxury behemoths like LVMH engage lawyers, spending as much as $17 million annually to take action against counterfeiting.[56] Companies have also employed technology to authenticate products and destroy fake goods.

The Digitization of Luxury

Luxury brands initially resisted ecommerce because of the perception that digitization would lessen feelings of exclusivity and accessibility. More recently, however, they have embraced ecommerce. With the shuttering of luxury boutiques due to COVID-19, shoppers who previously did not consider ecommerce interactions have learned to appreciate the personalized convenience. Technology and ecommerce also made it possible for luxury brands to acquire new affluent consumers who could not previously access traditional physical luxury channels because of their geographic location. Kering CFO Jean-Marc Duplaix called COVID-19 "a catalyst for . . . the rapid development of ecommerce."[57] Online luxury shopping was growing in 2019, but the growth was exponential in 2020. New technology services proliferated during the pandemic, including new digital payment methods, sales associate tools, and consumer-facing apps.

Farfetch, one of the leading global technology platforms for the luxury fashion industry, launched in 2008. It started as an ecommerce marketplace for luxury boutiques around the world, but today it connects customers in over 190 countries and supports over 1,200 brands, boutiques, and department stores. During Q2 of 2020, when many physical stores were closed or offered limited availability, Farfetch revenues surged by 48% year over year. The growth was driven by 500,000 new customers.[58] Farfetch benefited on two fronts: being an online platform, and the glut of inventory on the market.

One cause for concern, however, is that Farfetch has offered deeper discounts than online rivals, generally considered to be bad for luxury in the long term, but possibly prudent because of the economic crisis during the pandemic. Despite the growth in ecommerce, digital leaders like Farfetch and Yoox Net-a-Porter have difficulty making multibrand ecommerce profitable.

Mytheresa, another online retailer, has generally avoided the discount path and has managed profitability by paying attention to consumer metrics. Customer acquisition costs can be very high and not return adequate results, whereas focusing on high-value customer retention can deliver profitable outcomes. Mytheresa makes these kinds of trade-offs by utilizing customer lifetime value metrics. Sophisticated analyses tie investments to customers who will bring long-term value, and avoid aspirational customers who may buy one low-margin or trendy item and never return. They employ dynamic models that record, for example, which specific products people buy, when, and in what order to predict whether the shopper would be likely to return to the website. Unlike other ecommerce sites that feature endless assortments, Mytheresa is more laser focused. This strategy allows it to reduce operational expenses like photography requirements, inventory control, and marketing expenses.

Other ecommerce retailers have taken different approaches. Initially, ecommerce pioneer Net-a-Porter took an editorial/content approach, hoping to engage the customer with fashion advice and suggestions, follow influencers, and then facilitate the purchase process straight from the content. Mytheresa's approach uses the ecommerce platform to make things more convenient. These different approaches are similar to the divergences in China, where Alibaba takes the "kill time" approach and JD.com takes more of a "save time" approach. Moda Operandi is a multibrand designer retailer that lets customers preorder the latest ready-to-wear fashion right off the runway before it is available anywhere else.

Conclusion

Luxury continues to be a viable way to compete in a competitive retail world. While historically most high-end luxury retailers relied on the power of their exclusive, prestigious product brand names, this is no longer sufficient. These retailers have to continue to leverage their strengths while acknowledging changing consumer demands.

Most luxury retailers are experimenting with offering novel and desirable customer experiences that offer different types of luxury advantages. Although the central premise of luxury is scarcity and exclusivity, changes in consumer behavior are forcing luxury retailers to embrace the digital age. New luxury retailers like Yoox Net-a-Porter, Mytheresa, and Farfetch are making great strides, and most of the traditional retailers are developing ecommerce strategies of their own.

The critical strategy with respect to the lure of low price, though, will be to resist discounting and lowering prices as much as possible. Vigilant control of counterfeiting is also critical.

Chapter 6

Compete on Customer Experience
The Lure of Emotional and Sensory Engagement

In This Chapter: Kahn Retailing Success Strategy
- Retailers Whose Leadership Value Is to Offer Unique Customer Experiences
- Retailers Offering Great Customer Experiences as Their Second Leadership Quadrant

Most retail experts believe that even with massive growth in online shopping, brick-and-mortar retail stores are not going away. Even Amazon is hedging its bets and getting into physical stores.

Stores still serve a critical purpose: They allow customers to touch and feel a product, and to see it in real life. They provide social interaction with knowledgeable store associates. And they provide immediate ownership of purchased items.

Physical stores, though, will morph in response to changes in shopping behavior. Highly compelling in-store customer experiences will become more important as shoppers require additional reasons to visit. Brick-and-mortar retail space will evolve to include other experiences that complement shopping. And in-store technology will get better and better (and cheaper), while stores may start to include creative use of VR, AR, and real-time AI-driven algorithms that allow retailers to actively respond to customers' preferences and past behaviors.

Retailers that have prioritized the physical-store customer experience to create strategic differential advantages naturally fall into two categories.

First are the retailers that prioritize leadership in the Experiential quadrant as their chief strategic differentiation, then build on this leadership to maintain excellence in a second quadrant. One example is Eataly, whose stated mission is "to create a place to learn about food, and through food, to learn about life." Building on this unique experience that includes cooking schools, restaurants, and gourmet food markets, Eataly offers leadership in the Product Brand quadrant by offering exclusive specialty foods from regional Italian producers.

Others prioritize customer experience by recognizing the dynamic or changing aspect of the shopping experience, and hence the seasonality of the experiences becomes the reason to visit the store. One example is the pop-up retailers that offer temporary stores to create interest, like Spirit Halloween. Christmas stores do this as well.

The second category of retailers is those that build leadership strategies in a different quadrant, then build on those leadership qualities to offer differentiating customer experiences. Examples include retailers like Costco, with its club membership model, or T.J.Maxx, with its off-price strategy. Both retailers differentiate with a low-price strategy, but bring customers into their stores for the fun of a treasure hunt experience—although these two retailers define treasure hunt differently.

Other retailers that build on a different leadership strategy but then leverage that to create awe-inspiring customer experiences include Sephora, whose loyalty program differentiates it in the Frictionless quadrant through its efforts to collect customer data and use that information to create a peerless in-store customer experience.

Retailers Whose Leadership Value Is to Offer Unique Customer Experiences

Part of the allure of unique experiences is that they are special and, therefore, not always available. Thus, like luxury strategies, these

Figure 6.1. Plotting Unique Customer Experiences on the Kahn Retailing Success Matrix

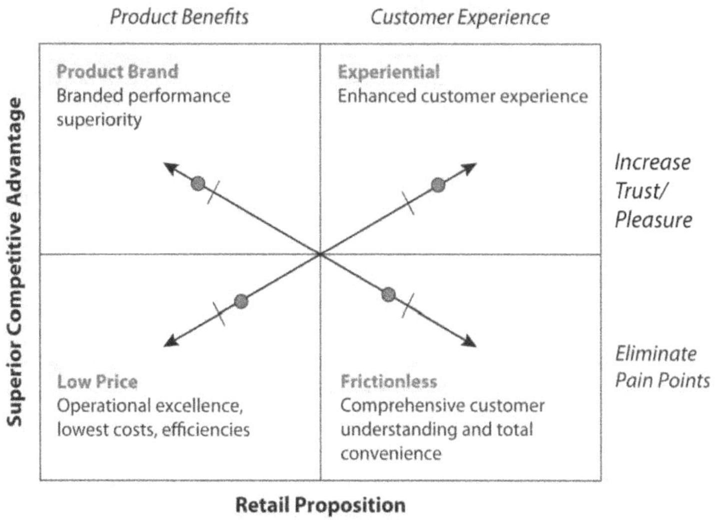

	Product Benefits	Customer Experience	

Product Brand
Branded performance
superiority

Experiential
Enhanced customer experience

Increase Trust/ Pleasure

Low Price
Operational excellence,
lowest costs, efficiencies

Frictionless
Comprehensive customer
understanding and total
convenience

Eliminate Pain Points

Superior Competitive Advantage

Retail Proposition

experiential retailers often do not meet fair value in the Frictionless quadrant and may not in Low Price either. Their leadership is first in the Experiential quadrant and then frequently followed by differentiated branded product. These ideas are plotted in figure 6.1.

Eataly

Eataly is a food emporium that features fresh meats, cheese, seafood, an on-site bakery, wines, fresh pasta, an espresso bar, and gourmet Italian specialty products, as well as full-service restaurants and a cooking school headed up by local celebrity chefs. There are currently only about three dozen locations worldwide, though the goal is to eventually have one store in every world capital. Eataly has an online presence as well, but that is clearly not its priority: As shown in figure 6.1, convenience and accessibility are not its central objectives. While Eataly and other food emporiums have suffered during the pandemic because their premise is counter to social distancing and depends on tourism, there is hope they can spring back, while limited outdoor seating and delivery services provide a stop-gap solution.

Oscar Farinetti started Eataly in Turin, Italy, in January 2007. He had been involved with the Slow Food movement for years and made connections with many small-scale food producers and artisans in Italy. He built on these connections to provide Italian specialty products for his establishments that aren't found anywhere else. In addition to the imported products and consistent with the Slow Food movement, 90% of the fresh products in Eataly establishments come from local areas. The emphasis on local products and local celebrity chefs make each Eataly unique.

The different components of the physical retail space provide complementary in-store consumer experiences, but they also provide synergy for the retailer. If the fresh product does not sell quickly enough, it can be used in the restaurants before it spoils. Having a cooking school on the premises allows customers to appreciate the fine qualities of the foods and drinks, which should increase demand. The restaurants create buzz and traffic that leads people to the products sold in the market. Eataly's store footprints are large; the newest one in Los Angeles is 67,000 square feet. Hence, the stores are often destinations.

Eataly is attempting to redefine retail. Rather than trying to maximize sales per square foot, which was the historical metric of success, Eataly is defining itself in terms of the customer experience. It is more like a Starbucks or Disneyland in terms of prioritizing experience, rather than a grocery store that tries to make profits by increasing frequency of purchase on low-margin items.

Pop-Up Stores: Spirit Halloween

Another unique concept is the pop-up store, and Spirit Halloween was one of the first exponents of this in 1983. Spirit operates just the two months before Halloween each year—but those two months are lucrative, generating over $100 million in annual revenues. It's a tricky model because every year the store has to find new locations, fully staff those locations, and get merchandise in place. Spirit opened roughly 1,300 temporary shops throughout the United States and Canada in 2017.

The idea behind a pop-up is temporary retail space that sells merchandise of any kind. They come in all shapes and sizes and are usually located in high foot-traffic areas. They can stay open from one day to three months. Although there are many reasons to open a pop-up, it is common to see them during holidays or when a brand is launching a new product. They offer uniqueness and novelty. As covered in chapter 5, luxury brands have seen the benefit of opening pop-up stores to help re-create their brand mystique.

Pop-ups have benefited from the closing of many more traditional brick-and-mortar stores. It's much easier now to find a vacant spot in busy neighborhoods that will be the right size for different uses. It's a win for landlords too, as they take in rent for a space that would otherwise be empty. And pop-ups are usually designed to be fun, so they tend to bring traffic to the neighborhood.

Retailers Offering Great Customer Experiences as Their Second Leadership Quadrant

The second group of retailers that differentiate on customer experience do so by building on a different primary leadership value. Although the strategies are different, Costco and T.J.Maxx (and other off-price retailers like Ross Stores and Burlington) are successful examples. Their critical differential advantage is leadership in the Low Price quadrant, but they marry that strategy with an exciting treasure hunt in-store customer experience.

As an intrinsic part of this strategy, retailers do not hit fair value on branded product, either because they *cannot* advertise the brands they have by contract with those brands (off-price retailers) or because by design they offer limited breadth in product assortment (Costco). It is, incidentally, this limitation that is the reason for the treasure

Figure 6.2. The Treasure Hunt Model on the Kahn Retailing Success Matrix

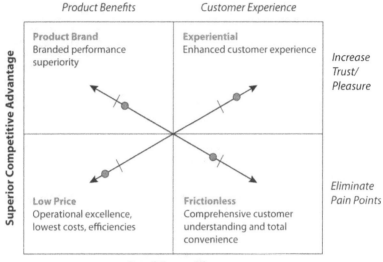

Product Benefits   *Customer Experience*

Product Brand
Branded performance
superiority

Experiential
Enhanced customer experience

*Increase
Trust/
Pleasure*

Low Price
Operational excellence,
lowest costs, efficiencies

Frictionless
Comprehensive customer
understanding and total
convenience

*Eliminate
Pain Points*

Superior Competitive Advantage

Retail Proposition

hunt excitement. Further, because their models depend so much on the physical store, they have not prioritized the Frictionless quadrant and are either playing catch-up (Costco) or deprioritizing it (off-price). These ideas are plotted on the Kahn Retailing Success Matrix in figure 6.2.

Costco

The first Costco warehouse started in 1983 in Seattle as a membership club. Costco uses its buying clout to get great prices on items and then passes those cost savings on to its customers. In addition to having to pay an annual membership fee in order to shop, customers shop in warehouses where products are displayed on shipping pallets, and they have to buy in larger quantities than they would in a regular supermarket. In return, they are guaranteed the lowest prices in the market. This model attracts small businesses as well as individual consumers.

A typical Costco warehouse stocks about 4,000 items, whereas a Walmart supercenter might carry 140,000 products. As a result, Costco carries only a limited number of brands in any particular category and offers no variety in sizes. The company runs lean, with overhead costs at about 10% of revenue and profit margins at about 2%. The annual membership fees account for 80% of gross margin and 70% of operating income. Costco has over 100 million cardholders.

Costco's Leadership Strengths:
Low Price and Customer Experience

Primarily, Costco is seen as a low-price leader. In 2017, a price comparison by JP Morgan in supermarket categories found that Costco prices on a per-unit basis were 30% cheaper than Walmart and 14% cheaper than Aldi, although Costco requires bulk purchases and the other supermarkets do not.[59]

Costco builds on this low-price advantage by offering a unique customer experience that serves to further motivate loyalty. This unique shopping experience occurs because customers are never quite sure what products will be offered at any time. Up to one-fifth of Costco's stock is offered for a limited time only, and these items may be kept in the stores for only one week. Because of the uncertainty in assortment options, Costco trains customers to buy something they like *when they see it*—because the next time they come, it probably won't be there.

Costco store experiences have also been exemplified by its tasting stations, which make the store feel like a party. In-store associates pass out trays of samples, supporting the social aspect of the store. (In-store sampling has been curtailed amid the pandemic.) The stores also draw customers into the physical plant because the warehouses sell gas at low prices.

None of these physical-store experiences—the treasure hunt, product sampling, or filling a car up with gas—can be adequately had online, so Costco has historically been a laggard in that space.

Costco Looks to Reach Fair Value in the Other Quadrants: Brand and Online

In the Product Brand quadrant, even though Costco offers a limited assortment, it is possible for it to achieve fair value for several reasons. First, the limited assortment can offer excitement in the form of a treasure hunt. Second, in a world of far too many choices, having a limited choice of high-quality goods may actually be beneficial; Costco has a reputation for carrying high-quality brands, so its limited assortment is viewed almost as a curated assortment, where the customer cannot go wrong. Finally, Costco's product image is strong because of its respected private-label Kirkland Signature brand.

Since 1995, Costco has used its Kirkland Signature products to attract shoppers. The brand is very high quality with a low price. About 25% of annual sales come from Kirkland products, and that percentage is growing. Further, Costco uses the possibility of its introducing a Kirkland product as incentive to make sure the national brands are selling at their lowest prices.

When Costco considers developing new products under the Kirkland brand, it looks for products that are top sellers that it believes can be sold for at least 20% less. If Costco decides to develop a private-label version, it looks to do so without eroding quality, and it is careful to make products that are slightly different from branded versions.

Costco plays fair; before going with a private brand, it gives the brand-name supplier the chance to make the Kirkland version too. For example, Costco asked P&G (Pampers) and Kimberly-Clark (Huggies) to make private Kirkland-branded diapers. Kimberly-Clark agreed, and Huggies is the only branded version sold on Costco shelves, in addition to the Kirkland brand.

In the Frictionless quadrant, Costco is playing catch-up. Although it has a strong and sticky membership base, it has two liabilities that suggest it is vulnerable in this quadrant. First, a 2017 Morgan Stanley study estimated that almost half of Costco shoppers are also members of Amazon Prime.[60]

Second, Costco has been slow to respond to the ecommerce threat, although this has definitely changed some since COVID-19 accelerated growth in the ecommerce area. Recently, Costco grocery partnered with Instacart to offer one-day delivery of fresh groceries. It also offers a limited number of "buy online, pick up in the store" items. Costco also launched CostcoGrocery, a service that offers two-day delivery on shelf-stable products ordered through its website.

Costco's Future

Costco was generally one of the stronger retailers coming into, and even during, COVID-19. Costco's gross annual profit was $19.8 billion in 2019, a 7.5% increase over 2018. And being an essential retailer, Costco was generally helped during the first two quarters of 2020. Even when restrictions curtailed foot traffic, Costco was less affected than other retailers, as its operating profit is primarily derived from membership sales (and its membership retention rate is about 90%).[61]

Growth for Costco will come from ecommerce and global expansion. Ecommerce at Costco increased 64.5% in Q3 of 2020 and now represents about 10% of total sales.[62] Costco acquired Innovel Solutions, a logistics company, for $1 billion, to help with deliveries of major appliances. Costco can now offer one-day delivery of fresh groceries, two-day delivery of dry groceries, and pharmacy home delivery.

Globally, in 2019 Costco warehouses were located in only 10 countries. A Costco warehouse opened in China in 2019 to tremendous success, and more stores are planned for the future.

T.J.Maxx, Burlington, and Ross Stores

T.J.Maxx, Burlington, and Ross Stores are all retailers that have been identified as "off-price," and they all follow a similar model. They buy products in bulk at good prices, then pass on those prices to consumers. They are "everyday low price" and do not discount. They make profits from volume; they sell lots of goods and they sell them fast.

These retailers buy two types of products for their stores: (1) true closeout products (i.e., branded products created to sell at full price in other stores but didn't sell for one reason or another) and (2) products made specifically for the off-price channel, designed to be sold at discounted prices.

The first group is true bargains, often selling at 20% to 60% below retail price, and contributes to the treasure hunt feel. Unlike at Costco, in these stores there are only a few of any specific designs and/or sizes in each store, but the stores offer broad assortments with tons of variety that changes frequently.

These retailers are "fashion" retailers; they are not in the business of selling other retailers' losing bets. They have large numbers of buyers who study the trends. Unlike traditional fashion retailers, they don't have to make a bet at the beginning of the season; rather, they can buy closed-out products and samples during the season when they have better evidence about what is selling.

The key to success with these retailers is to be attuned to fashion. They invest in significant buyer training. The buyers buy most weeks of the year (not just seasonably), and they are negotiating significant amounts of money in each transaction. Knowing when to buy is as important as what to buy. Most of their items turn over quickly.

The second group of products—those specifically made for these chains—can also follow fashion trends quickly. If the off-price buyers see a hot trend, they can negotiate with manufacturers to have merchandise made for them directly. Some vendors will produce an excess of hot items knowing that the off-price buyers will take them. The advantage to the vendors is that the off-price retailers will buy in volume, which will help economies of scale. And the off-price retailers will spread that product across their stores so there is not a lot of supply in any one place. These arrangements are typically not publicized, which is beneficial for both.

All of these stores have a large physical footprint, which makes for broad, but not deep, assortments. T.J.Maxx stores, for example, may cover 23,000 square feet of retail space. It sources from more than 16,000 vendors around the world. Burlington stores are even bigger, sometimes as large as 80,000 square feet, but they are being scaled back to probably half of that.

Customers of off-price retailers come to the store not knowing what to expect, but they know that if they find a great bargain, they have to buy it right away. This provides a real sense of urgency and excitement, which helps to turn over the inventory quickly. Fast-turning inventory increases the frequency at which consumers come into the store.

No Plans for Online Platforms

This is a shopping experience that doesn't translate easily to online. From the consumer side, the shopping experience would not convert to a small computer screen (or mobile phone). In a physical store, you can scan, see things in your peripheral vision, and find treasures accidentally. Online search is far more focused.

From the retailer side, there are disincentives to try to replicate the process online because of rapid turnover in stores. Photographing rapidly changing inventory would be difficult, and without an extensive description of each of the items, seeing and trying on the product physically in the stores becomes more important. To the degree it is difficult to fully and quickly describe the items, returns are a bigger issue—let alone the costs of delivery, which in this model the consumer bears. Further, manufacturers will not allow easy identification of their brand products, so online search is prohibited. All of this makes it difficult to see how this type of retailing will successfully move online.

Successful Numbers

This sector is posting strong results, with steady sales and earnings growth. Although this segment is successful, the off-price model has been hard to get right; many have failed in the past. Syms overextended, Loehmann's couldn't scale, Century 21 is good but small and recently closed its stores (another casualty of COVID-19), and Filene's Basement couldn't scale and found itself overextended.

The key to success is the supply chain and distribution. A successful retailer in this model needs huge, fully automated distribution centers in the right places. It needs to buy the product from all over the world and then distribute it efficiently and effectively to all of its stores. Most of these retailers have a "door to floor" approach, eliminating the need for backroom storage. It is key to have rapid turnover of inventory in the stores, to keep the assortment fresh, and to encourage consumers to keep coming back. They also need to be able to store a lot of inventory if necessary.

Risks to the Model in the Future

Although this model has been very successful for the big three—T.J.Maxx, Ross, and Burlington—success brings competition, and large department stores are taking note. They are prioritizing their own off-price offerings and opening up new stores. And as technology and AI make it easier to predict what consumers will want, demand forecasts should be more accurate, and there may be less full-price inventory for sale.

Some analysts have speculated that competition may emerge from online secondhand retailers like thredUP and Everything But The House. But that seems unlikely for many reasons. First, secondhand clothing has a time lag, which may matter for fashionistas. Second, some consumers don't like the idea of wearing clothing that strangers have worn. Probably more important, though, are the supply-side costs like shipping, inventory, distribution, photography, and returns, which would make it difficult for this type of channel to compete effectively.

How COVID-19 Affected Off-Price Stores

T.J.Maxx, Ross, and Burlington took a big hit as the pandemic took hold, as all of their stores physically closed. But none changed strategies materially on ecommerce.

The commitment to limited ecommerce is motivated by two reasons: First, the easiness of searching online would limit big brands' desire to be associated with these off-price retailers. Second, online sales cannibalize in-store sales without providing the in-store experience—and the in-store experience is *the point* of the shopping trip.

Consistent with that philosophy, when these stores reopened, mostly in early June 2020, loyal consumers flooded them. Janine Stichter, an analyst who covers retail for the Jefferies Financial Group, defines the shopping behavior observed at these off-price retailers as an unpredictable journey. And for the loyal consumers, the lockdown only magnified their desire to get back into the stores. She called the behavior "shoptimism," which she defined as a type of "retail therapy" that turns shopping into a form of comfort and satisfaction, and an act of faith toward a more normal future.[63] T.J.Maxx has the most developed online presence in the category, and that accounts for only 2% of its sales.[64]

Other Retailers Building Strong Customer Experiences on Other Leadership Strengths

Finally, other retailers provide amazing customer experiences based on strengths in other quadrants. Sephora built a strong loyalty program and has leveraged that online expertise to craft a can't-miss store experience. Sephora excels at customer experience, offers very strong brands, and hits fair value on price. The aim is to motivate on value rather than on discounting. These ideas are plotted in figure 6.3.

Sephora

Sephora, owned by LVMH, is a fully integrated omnichannel experience with a very loyal customer base. The store is a makeup playground. Consumers come into the store to experiment with makeup, skin-care products, perfumes, and anything beauty related. The store associates are there to help and educate. They are not on commission.

The in-store experience is connected with customers' online accounts, so there is a record of previous purchases, making color

Figure 6.3. Plotting In-Store Customer Experience on the Kahn Retailing Success Matrix

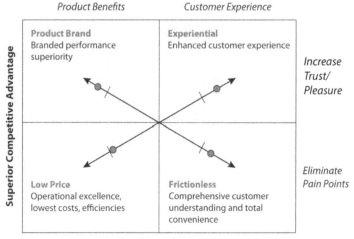

Product Benefits   *Customer Experience*

Superior Competitive Advantage

Product Brand
Branded performance
superiority

Experiential
Enhanced customer experience

Increase Trust/ Pleasure

Low Price
Operational excellence,
lowest costs, efficiencies

Frictionless
Comprehensive customer
understanding and total
convenience

Eliminate Pain Points

Retail Proposition

matches easy to reproduce. Also, all purchases are recorded to a robust loyalty program, which not only allows for appropriate recommendations and announcements of personalized new products, but also awards bonus points that lead to fun beauty gifts that keep the customer addicted.

Sephora's combination of a well-run loyalty program (with well-timed and well-designed bonus gifts) and a fun in-store environment is intoxicating. The stores are always crowded, and I have personally seen women standing outside of a closed Sephora store, literally crying that they didn't make it there in time.

Although an online experience may be useful for repurchasing stock items, the beauty purchase is especially conducive to an in-store experience, as most people like to try on products before buying. Of course, changes due to the pandemic have affected and will continue to affect the in-store experience. At least for the foreseeable future, Sephora will not allow shoppers to test products. How this change affects shopping remains to be seen. For most beauty-industry markets, even though a robust online community exists, in-store shopping typically accounts for up to 85% of purchases on average. Even for Gen Z, in-store purchases account for about 60% of overall purchases.[65]

Historically, Sephora has always experimented with new concepts to keep in-store environments novel and fresh. That some of these involved technology will be especially useful in the changed environment. For example, in 2015 it introduced the TIP (Teach, Inspire, Play) concept that featured makeup classes with a completely interactive experience designed for innovation and experimentation. Makeup stations in the store had sensory and color technology to help customers learn about new possibilities. Sephora also experiments with AR, which allows customers to try on makeup virtually. There will be a bigger focus on mobile as well for virtual testers. These "use your own device" options can help shoppers experiment with new products and colors.

The Sephora experience is also about social interaction. In its robust Beauty Insider community, for example, customers talk with each other about products and fashion. In the first few months after its launch, the program had 100,000 live chats, and more than 20,000 photos were shared.

Sephora has also opened small Sephora Studio stores, which are designed to have a neighborhood feel. Here the emphasis is on intimacy and building relationships between the customer and store associates, which encourages even more repeat visits.

Is Sephora Vulnerable to Amazon?

Amazon is rumored to be looking at beauty in addition to fashion. But until Amazon prioritizes the experiential and social in-store experience that Sephora excels at, Sephora's customers will likely stay put.

In addition to Amazon, plenty of other competition exists in this segment. The department stores historically owned a lot of this market, especially at the higher end where Sephora competes. At the lower-price points, drugstores, supermarkets, and mass merchandisers can compete with better prices but have little opportunity for in-store experimentation. Ulta is doing extremely well in combining both high- and low-priced goods with a compelling in-store environment that includes salons and a strong loyalty program. There are also many startups eyeing this space, including Birchbox and the upcoming and fast-growing Glossier.

Conclusion

All retailers in this chapter have excelled in customer experience. As with branded products, each experience is unique, and that is the appeal. Like luxury, these experiences are special *because* they are hard to access, rare, or scarce—the opposite of the convenient and frictionless experience, Amazon's forte. Many of the retailers that prioritize physical customer experience do not prioritize online ecommerce, especially those that feature low prices (e.g., Costco and T.J.Maxx). Sephora and other beauty retailers will need to merge the online experience with the physical experience.

Of course, good ideas are always copied, so first, competition might be around the corner. Second, experiences that are considered fun, like the fashion shopping experience, might change over time. Finally, although currently not the case, VR could make these experiences reproducible at home.

As always, cost-benefit analysis will be necessary to measure whether the investment in in-store experiences delivers long-term returns. But at the very least, there is evidence that if retailers build the excitement, customers will come.

Chapter 7

Learning from "New Retail" in China

In This Chapter

- Alibaba (Taobao and Tmall), the largest ecommerce marketplace in China, is strong on low prices and is the leader in the Brand Product and Experiential quadrants.
- JD.com, the second-largest ecommerce marketplace (by gross merchandise value), is the largest online retailer in China, offers the best frictionless experience, and has the best control of counterfeiting.

This chapter benefits from the research, suggestions, and commentary provided by Yupeng Liu, Daniel Wu, and Genna Zimmer as part of an independent study course they completed under my supervision while they were Executive MBA students at the Wharton School at the University of Pennsylvania. I thank the Wharton School Global Fund, Wharton/Penn China Center, and the Baker Retailing Center for funding for our trip to China and for help in setting up our in-country interviews with the retailing industry experts.

This chapter also benefits from conversations I had in Beijing and Shanghai, China, with the following retailing executives:

- Frank Di (director of investments), Ada Yang (international corporate affairs), and David Liu (VP strategy) from PDD
- Yingming Zhao (president of JD fashion) and Belinda Chen (lifestyle, JD retail) from JD
- Alan Zong (investment director) and Xinxin Zhang (senior investment manager) from Alibaba
- Susan Sun (VP merchandising) and Jack Diao (GM for offline business) from VIP.com
- Alexis Bonhomme (VP of B2B for Greater China) from Farfetch

- Pinduoduo (PDD), the newcomer on the Chinese ecommerce landscape, is the second-largest ecommerce player (by number of users and order counts).[66] PDD entered the scene with a compelling low price but has also redefined the ecommerce shopping experience by emphasizing gamification and social interaction.

Alibaba's Freshippo (Hema) supermarkets popping up in the large cities in China are a great example of what Jack Ma, the cofounder of Alibaba, calls "new retail." With already more than 150 locations, Freshippo is a combination of supermarket, fresh-food restaurant, and online fulfillment center. With facial recognition payment processes, overhead conveyor belts that facilitate online orders, and 30-minute delivery options, this futuristic consumer-centric seamless blending of offline and online retailing maximizes consumer convenience. Ma's concept of "new retail" also brings entertainment, media, and gamification into the shopping experience. While Amazon and Walmart have certainly embraced omnichannel retailing, the approach in China takes it to a new level in efficiency and implementation.

The ecommerce market is much larger in China than anywhere else. According to China's national bureau of statistics, Chinese consumers spent $750 billion online in 2016,[67] more than was spent in the United States and United Kingdom combined. In addition, China is the pioneer in mobile commerce; in 2020, estimates are that mobile phones will account for 74% of total ecommerce.[68] Because of cultural differences, Chinese consumers have different shopping preferences, and the ecommerce market has evolved to cater to these differences. Alibaba has a dominating position in China (56% ecommerce market share in 2019[69]), giving it the market power to innovate. For these reasons, the Chinese ecommerce model serves as a roadmap for the future of retailing for the rest of the world.

Cultural Factors in China Lead to Differences in Shopping Behavior

Compared with American culture, which tends to be more individualistic and prioritizes individual goals, Chinese society is more collectivistic, and the Chinese care how their own actions affect the group. Chinese consumers, especially younger ones, thoroughly embrace social media and enjoy recommending products to their networks. More than 75% of Chinese internet users post online feedback on purchases at least once a month, compared with less than 20% of internet users in the United States.[70]

Another cultural difference in China that encourages the sharing of experiences and reviews is the concept of Mianzi (face), which dates back to the fourth century B.C. This concept of "saving face," referring to self-esteem, reputation, and social status, affects all actions in one's business and personal life. For example, Chinese consumers may have purchases sent to the office rather than to their home so that office colleagues can see what they bought. There is also the idea of "giving face," which refers to giving the other party a feeling of respect.

These cultural factors unique to the Chinese marketplace have helped shape China's ecommerce. Chinese consumers not only recommend more but are also more likely to purchase recommended products. Facilitating this social behavior is the pervasive use of the mobile payment systems WeChat and Alipay. These "super app" payment systems are combined with messaging platforms that allow conversations about purchases. In addition, the popularity of video blogs (vlogs) and livestreaming used by key opinion leaders has spawned the lucrative world of interactive "shoppertainment."

The Popularity of Super Apps: WeChat and Alipay

WeChat, owned by Tencent, has more than a billion monthly users. It not only offers a texting network but also allows users to do everything from making payments to booking flights and hotels to hailing a ride. (For comparison, in the United States, these activities would require separate apps.) Importantly, WeChat facilitates purchasing products directly from the app. Similarly, Alibaba's Taobao, a consumer-to-consumer (C2C) marketplace comparable to eBay, offers social interaction and entertainment and is linked to the app Alipay, a digital mobile wallet. The two systems, WeChat and Alipay, are independent and represent a combined 90% of the payment market in China.[71]

Unlike in the United States, where payment is still dominated by credit and debit cards, the growth of mobile payment in China has been swift. The research firm eMarketer projects that by 2021, 79.3% of smartphone users in China will be using mobile phone payment, while the figure in the United States is projected to be only 30.8% and only 22% in Germany.[72] Use of mobile payment systems helps keep retail prices low because the merchant gets a higher percentage of the payment than for credit card purchases.

Given the ease of these super apps, the Chinese are more likely to go straight to Taobao or WeChat's marketplaces than to a brand's website. In fact, on mobile devices, apps from just four companies—Baidu, Tencent, Alibaba, and Touttiao (the owner of TikTok)—occupied 70% of total users' active time on mobile phones in China in 2019.[73] And since these apps are connected to the consumers' messaging networks, shoppers are also more likely to share their experiences.

Unlike on Amazon, whose 1-Click shopping has made the process even easier in the United States, many Chinese think of shopping as an adventure during which they can "kill time." And whereas in the United States most shoppers associate the treasure hunt experience with the physical-store environment, the Chinese have mastered the online treasure hunt experience.

The Chinese consumer is willing to spend hours experiencing entertainment, discovery, and social engagement while shopping. This merging of social networking and online shopping functionality has been dubbed "social commerce." Consumers spend almost 30 minutes a day on Alibaba's Taobao, three times longer than the typical American spends on Amazon. Since the Chinese are more willing to explore and therefore provide more data, ecommerce retailers can innovate with multimedia and sophisticated algorithms that build on shoppers' past purchases and preferences, and they can better predict new content that will engage shoppers and spur purchasing.

Shoppertainment: A New Way to Drive Retail Sales

Social commerce will make up 11.6% of total retail ecommerce sales in 2020, with nearly one-third of mainland Chinese participating.[74] A big part of social commerce comes through vlogs where an influencer creates an information channel composed of short videos or livestreaming. In 2019, vlogs were followed by almost half of all internet users in China. Taobao, Tmall, JD.com, and VIP all rolled out their own vlog services by 2018.

These social commerce influencer channels provide shoppers with knowledge about products. People tune in to learn about skin care, beauty, snacks, or household products in a manner more similar to chatting with a friend than listening to a high-pressured sales pitch. To keep followers, the influencer's content must stay authentic and not be promotional. The combination of purchasing and video entertainment has been dubbed "shoppertainment." Shoppertainment is far different from the American formula of TV home shopping, such as HSN or QVC.

Several ecommerce and social media platform sites that allow for user-generated content have become popular. For example, Xiaohongshu, also known as the Little Red Book, is an online platform backed by Tencent and Alibaba. Its valuation reached about $5 billion in 2019, with more than 300 million registered users.[75] It started in 2013 as an online community that recommended overseas ecommerce sites for users in China, but in 2015–16 added ecommerce. It has become one of China's foremost fashion and luxury shopping platforms. People have likened the site to a combination of Pinterest and Instagram, wherein users can post videos or photos of products and reviews or blogs. When users create content that attracts a significant following, they can earn a commission by becoming influencers. When they become very popular, they are known as key opinion leaders (KOLs). Strict policies come with that label: KOLs have to register and submit a certification to obtain the right to post commercial information.

Little Red Book makes a distinction between KOLs, who typically get commissions, and KOCs (key opinion customers), who are not paid, although they may receive free products. KOLs are not celebrities first: They are self-made influencers, and they typically have many millions of followers. They livestream daily and encourage their followers to chat with them. Building on their success, some KOLs have recently opened their own offline stores. KOCs, on the other hand, are everyday consumers who share experiences on social media and typically have an audience of only several hundred to a few thousand. Because they are not paid, they may seem more authentic.

Another popular site for shoppertainment is Douyin, also known as TikTok in the United States, which has more than 800 million users worldwide. Whereas Little Red Book tends to be more utilitarian, Douyin is more entertaining. TikTok has moved overseas and has become a smash hit in many countries. In China, because of its link to the Alibaba sites of Taobao and Tmall, it relies heavily on ecommerce. Every user is different on Douyin, which makes money on advertisement revenues and click-through rates on TaoBao.

Alibaba's Singles' Day and the Rapid Growth of Livestreaming

The growth of ecommerce and social commerce has been facilitated through the very popular shopping event called Singles' Day, November 11, which Alibaba established as a shopping event in 2009. The idea was to encourage single people to shop for themselves on Alibaba's shopping marketplace, Taobao, as an antidote to Valentine's Day and its emphasis on couples. To entice them to shop, Taobao offered discounts up to 50%. Singles' Day has grown to become the largest online shopping day in the world.

In 2019, Alibaba's Singles' Day broke records. Total sales hit nearly $38.3 billion in gross merchandise value, more than twice the amount of 2018's Black Friday, Cyber Monday, and Amazon Prime Day combined. Taobao Live reached 35 million views.[76]

Though there are obvious potential downsides—including consumers delaying their purchases or risking making consumers too price-sensitive the rest of the year—Singles' Day has become an undoubted success. In addition to incredible sales revenues, Singles' Day helped popularize the use of livestreaming as a major channel combining entertainment and ecommerce. In 2019, for example, Kim Kardashian decided to introduce her new fragrance to Chinese consumers on Singles' Day by participating on a livestream channel with Viya, one of the top female KOLs in China with 40 million followers. She sold 15,000 bottles of perfume in minutes.[77]

Much of the growth in ecommerce in China has come from the third- and fourth-tier cities, which are less developed urban centers and rural areas. These consumers typically have fewer entertainment options, so they have more time to spend online. Livestreaming is especially popular because it ensures a level of authenticity. The ability to chat in the moment with KOLs increases relatability and provides instant feedback.

In 2020, livestreaming on social commerce became an even bigger phenomenon because of COVID-19. Even if quarantined fans had to stay home, they could video chat with their favorite influencers and purchase products online. In February 2020, Alibaba's Taobao Live platform grew more than sevenfold in first-time business customers, while PDD's livestreaming sessions grew fivefold from February to March 2020.

The Top Three Retailing Platforms Make Up 80% of the Ecommerce Market

The ecommerce market in China is forecasted to represent about 64% of the total Chinese retail sales market by 2023.[78] Given the relative lack of malls or physical retailing centers in third- and fourth-tier cities, ecommerce grew quickly as a replacement. When physical stores did open, they were built as "new retail," where physical and online transactions are seamlessly integrated, and logistics management processes control the inventory accordingly. In 2019, Chinese ecommerce spending was estimated at $1.9 trillion,[79] three times that of the US market.

As of May 2019, Alibaba, JD.com, and PDD were the leading ecommerce retailers in China, and together they represent nearly 80% of total online retail sales. Alibaba is by far the leader of the pack with 55.9% market share; JD.com is next with 16.7%; and PDD, the newcomer, has 7.3%. (As a comparison, eMarketer estimates Amazon's ecommerce market share in the United States to be 38% in 2020.)[80] The US retailers that entered China have since yielded to the strength of these Chinese companies. Amazon entered China in 2004 through the acquisition of Joyo, which was rebranded as Amazon China. While its initial market share was considerable, it eventually plunged, and in 2019 Amazon closed its marketplace business in China. Walmart sold its Chinese marketplace to JD.com in 2016, keeping a stake in JD.com. Google is also working with JD.com.

Plotting Chinese Retailers on the Kahn Retailing Success Matrix

To get an overview perspective, it is beneficial to plot each of the leading retailers' Two-Quadrant Winning Strategies on the Kahn Retailing Success Matrix (see figure 7.1). In viewing the figure, there are a few caveats to take into consideration. First, Alibaba is dominant in the market, giving it considerable market power, so it can choose to be dominant in any quadrant. The leadership quadrants I assigned to Alibaba follow from its stated strategies. Second, the Chinese consumer is very price sensitive. In addition, Singles' Day, in which many retailers participate, trains consumers to shop for deep discounts, which increases price sensitivity throughout the year. Fair value in the Low Price quadrant is generally high, guaranteeing a lot of price competition.

Figure 7.1. Two-Quadrant Winning Strategies

Alibaba

Product/Brand	Experiential
Low Price	Frictionless

JD.com

Product/Brand	Experiential
Low Price	Frictionless

Pinduoduo Inc.

Product/Brand	Experiential
Low Price	Frictionless

As the figure shows, for Alibaba (which owns two marketplace platforms: Taobao and Tmall), its stated Two-Quadrant Winning Strategy starts in experience. Taobao literally means "search for treasure," and Alibaba offers shoppers a personalized, customized discovery experience whenever they frequent either site. Alibaba builds on that strong customer experience to offer the best in brands through Tmall, which is business-to-consumer (B2C), and extensive product assortment through Taobao, which is C2C and small businesses, similar to eBay. Alibaba is a clear leader in the Product Brand quadrant as well. Given its size and scale, it can always deliver to ever-increasing fair-value expectations on low price and frictionless.

JD, which invested heavily in building its own supply chain and delivery fleet, can ensure a smooth, frictionless customer experience for product delivery. This makes JD.com the king of frictionless in China, and the largest ecommerce retailer. Building on that leadership advantage, it offers consumers a more curated product assortment with less concern about counterfeiting. This gives it a second leadership advantage in the Product Brand quadrant for shoppers who want to save time.

Finally, Pinduoduo (PDD) (literally "together more savings, more fun") has a slogan of "Value and Happiness for Everyone." This clearly translates to a Two-Quadrant Winning Strategy that starts in the Low-Price quadrant and builds on that leadership advantage to offer a superior shopping experience.

Alibaba Leads on Experience and Offers Superior Brand and Product Assortment

In 1999, Ma launched Alibaba with a small group of friends. The initial goal was to establish a business-to-business (B2B) marketplace that would connect international buyers, particularly from the United States, with Chinese manufacturers. Alibaba was originally designed to deliver to small Chinese businesses an "open sesame" to world trade, referencing "Ali Baba and the Forty Thieves," the folktale in *One Thousand and One Nights*.

Although Alibaba has the largest share of online retail sales, it is not a retailer. It is an online platform, more like a mall, for other retailers to sell. While Alibaba started as a traditional ecommerce company, it now has a range of businesses, including financial (Alipay) and logistics services, digital media, and cloud computing. The number of active consumers across Alibaba's online shopping properties is estimated to be over 700 million as of Q4 2019,[81] bigger than the population of the United States.

Alibaba Motivates Consumers to "Kill Time"
What drives consumers to Alibaba is the chance for discovery. Alibaba's algorithms help shape the ecommerce experience, so consumers are likely to find something they like, and maybe weren't even looking for.

Alibaba's combination of product assortments, availability of popular brands, a treasure hunt experience powered by AI, and the ease of the "super app" providing entertainment and easy payment through Alipay encourages consumers to "kill time" on the Taobao app. A majority of transactions are on mobile. Overall, the experience is sticky, because there is always something new.

Alibaba Compared with Amazon

Unlike Amazon, Alibaba itself does not carry inventory or buy and sell merchandise, and only recently has begun to participate in logistics such as sourcing, storage, and shipping.[82] Primarily, Alibaba creates software platforms that facilitate the exchange of goods and services. On the retailing side, revenues come from advertising dollars that allow brands to be better featured on the platform or within the site's internal search engine (a model that resembles Google's core business). In China, the largest search engine is Baidu, but that search engine is blocked from searching Taobao and Tmall, so the only way to see what Tmall and Taobao have available is to go directly to their pages. While Taobao does not charge a fee for transactions, there are commission fees for sellers on Tmall. In addition, sellers that maintain a storefront on their platform must pay a deposit and annual fees.

Since Alibaba is not a first-party retailer, it does not compete directly with the brands that are sold on its platform, as Amazon does. And since its revenue model focuses on advertising dollars, it is not interested in changing brands into commodities, but rather helping build brand equity. Alibaba has lower revenues than Amazon, but it has higher operating margins and profit margins in its retail businesses. Alibaba can offer low prices because of efficient operations and the strategic use of data. The ecosystem is based on trust, and there are rules to ensure honorable behavior.

Ma's philosophy was quoted by the *Wall Street Journal*: "We know well we haven't survived because our strategies are farsighted and brilliant, or because our execution is perfect, but because for 15 years we have persevered in our mission of 'making it easier to do business across the world,' because we have insisted on a 'customer first' value system, because we have persisted in believing in the future, and because we have insisted that normal people can do extraordinary things."[83]

Taobao (literally "search for treasure")

Alibaba has two platforms in China: Taobao, a C2C site similar to eBay, and Tmall, a B2C third-party marketplace. Alibaba also has AliExpress, an international B2C site that offers goods at factory prices without a minimum order size to international shoppers, mainly in the United States, Russia, Brazil, and Spain.

Taobao was launched in 2003 to compete with Ebay Eachnet, China's online auction leader at the time. Taobao is currently the world's biggest online shopping website and in 2016 had over 1 billion product listings. Taobao is not about big brands but is rather a platform for small businesses and individual entrepreneurs to sell to consumers.

Taobao creates shopping excitement for its consumers through colorful graphics and creative layouts, and through deals and limited promotions that help escalate excitement.

Taobao is also the "super app" mentioned earlier that facilitates easy payment and encourages social media posts about purchases. Livestreaming and vlogs increase the entertainment value associated with the site, while consumers are also driven by the treasure hunt experience. Sophisticated AI algorithms learn consumers' preferences and browsing behavior and can always optimize and individualize the shopping experience.

Tmall Offers Well-Known Brands

If Chinese consumers want to buy well-known brands, they go to Alibaba's Tmall, established in 2008. Tmall is the world's second-largest ecommerce website after Taobao and offers many well-known brands. US brands like Procter & Gamble, Estée Lauder, Mars, Mattel, Apple, Microsoft, Bose, NBA Nike, Gap, Levi Strauss & Co., Disney, New Balance, and Johnson & Johnson partner with Tmall. Tmall has higher price points compared with Taobao, and consumers generally trust its product quality. Brands that sell on Tmall can open an online store with the look and feel of their brand, and they have total control of the customer experience.

Even a digitally native brand like Allbirds, which has famously resisted selling on Amazon, has offered its shoes on Tmall. Allbirds executives have commented on how different the shopping experience for their shoes has been in China compared with that of the United States. In China, 95% of Allbirds sales on Tmall came on mobile, while in the United States that figure is about 50%.[84] Also, 80% of the consumers who purchase Allbirds products on Tmall leave feedback for other consumers; they share photos of items they bought and of themselves wearing the shoes.

For luxury brands and premium brands, Tmall offers the Luxury Pavilion. This dedicated channel allows luxury retailers to offer shoppers the same personalized experiences they could get from brick-and-mortar stores, such as free engraving or embossing, gift wrapping, or customized card services. Chinese consumers are big purchasers of luxury products: McKinsey estimates that they will make up 40% of the world's spending on luxury goods by 2025.[85] But many luxury companies do not have a physical presence in China and rely entirely on Tmall and Pavilion to reach their target consumers, especially in third- or fourth-tier cities. This partnership with Pavilion allows luxury brands to keep their exclusivity but to utilize the scale and size of Tmall.

Unlike Amazon, Tmall shares all data with individual brands, reducing guesswork and inventory uncertainties and providing opportunities to experiment. Tmall does not control the price but provides data for businesses to conduct price elasticity tests. Tmall analyzes brands it allows on its platform and uses new tech tools to crack down on counterfeit goods. Counterfeiting is handled through AI enforcement tools, to which brands have access.

Hema (Freshippo) Grocery Store: Alibaba's New Retail Strategy

As mentioned earlier, Hema—Alibaba's brick-and-mortar grocery stores, first launched in 2016—represents Alibaba's foray into "new retail," where the boundaries between online and offline retail disappear. All shopping is integrated, including logistics, data, payments, smart hardware, and more. The integration makes it easier for the customer to shop online or offline and is more efficient for the operator. At Hema, everything happens through the mobile app; shoppers can order online for home delivery, do in-store product research, and make payments.

Within the physical store, every item has a price tag and a corresponding barcode and QR code. The price tags are connected to the internet, which allows prices to change dynamically to reflect supply and demand. Shoppers can also use their phones to scan product codes and find out more information, from the product's producer to where it came from to when it arrived in the store.

The Hema stores serve as fulfillment and distribution centers for online orders, as the back of the stores provide warehousing. Workers in the store gather items and place them on overhead conveyor belts to the delivery center. Customers who live within a three-kilometer radius of the store can get home delivery within 30 minutes. One of the specialties of the Hema stores is the fresh seafood section. Customers choose their own seafood, which is flown in from all over the world, and they can have it delivered.

JD.com Has the Best Frictionless Platform and Offers a Curated Product Assortment

Richard Liu Qiangdong launched Jingdong (JD) in 1998 as a storefront selling magneto-optical in Beijing. It soon diversified into selling electronics, mobile phones, and computers. By 2008, JD.com began offering general merchandise in addition to electronics and became a multiproduct ecommerce platform.

JD.com formed a partnership with Tencent in 2014 and provided ecommerce retail access to the WeChat payment system. In 2016, JD .com and Walmart announced a strategic alliance. Google is also an investor, but most work with Google will remain outside of China, as Google's services are either blocked or unavailable. Of the three big players, JD.com's retail model is the most similar to Amazon's, as it allows first-party and third-party sellers on its platform.

JD.com Is King of "Frictionless" in China

Unlike Alibaba, JD invested heavily in building its own supply chain, and it owns its entire delivery fleet, right through the "last mile" delivery to the consumer. It owns the warehouses, distribution centers, and logistics, taking complete control over ensuring a smooth customer experience. This makes JD the king of "frictionless" in China. JD.com is the largest online direct sales ecommerce retailer in the country based on transaction value.

JD continues to invest in supply chain logistics and can offer same-day shipping in multiple first- and second-tier cities, ahead of Taobao and Tmall. Because it controls so much more of its own inventory, sourcing goods directly from suppliers and selling them on its platform (first-party sales), counterfeiting is much less of an issue on JD.com than on Taobao.

JD.com is also growing by extending to the lower-tier cities and rural markets. By 2018, JD had launched 7,000 delivery and pickup stations and 500 warehouses.[86] JD relies on drones, which it uses to reach outlying rural areas. JD is an early adopter when it comes to technology, which differentiates it from Alibaba. JD.com claims to be capable of delivering "over 90% of orders same or next day, with reach to 99% of China's population."[87]

Building Out Its Product Assortment

In 2010, JD.com launched a marketplace platform, allowing third-party sellers to transact on the site. JD executives have indicated that their strategy was to pick the best products within a category rather than having a massive selection, which is perhaps most similar to Costco's strategy. JD.com's strategy caters to shoppers who want to save time with a curated assortment and where authenticity can be guaranteed. JD prioritizes safety, trust, and quality over massive selection. Sellers can't come on JD.com's marketplace unless invited.

In the luxury sector, JD has partnered with Farfetch, the luxury ecommerce retailing platform that got its start by connecting local boutiques on its marketplace to global consumers. Farfetch China launched a flagship store on JD.com and acquired JD.com's

independent luxury shopping platform, Toplife. Farfetch uses JD
.com logistical capabilities to operate in the region. Through Farfetch,
JD.com's customers have access to a broad selection of luxury fash-
ion online and get the added security of authenticity guaranteed by
JD's control of inventory. JD is one of the largest shareholders in
Farfetch, and Liu sits on the marketplace's board (as of 2020).
(Alibaba has formed a joint venture with Yoox Net-a-Porter, the
largest online luxury retailer globally by revenue.)

In the important grocery sector, JD.com, like Alibaba, has
opened its own high-tech supermarkets called 7Fresh. The first
4,000-square-foot store opened in Beijing in 2018, getting 75% of its
turnover from fresh food.[88] The store uses analytics to match its product range to consumers' desires and uses technology to provide
additional information. Its plan is to offer smart shopping carts that
will allow consumers to shop hands-free and on the mobile app,
while payment technology will handle those processes. Similar to
Hema, 7Fresh can deliver orders within a five-kilometer radius
within 30 minutes. 7Fresh stores double as warehouses and distribution hubs, but unlike Alibaba, which relies on a network of third-
party logistics operations, JD has its own in-house services.

Accelerated Growth During COVID-19

Amid the onset of COVID-19 shutdowns in 2020, JD.com became a
go-to place to buy groceries. Overall revenue grew at a better-than-
expected rate, but the bread-and-butter electronics business suffered.
JD.com was in a better place to meet the surge in demand for essential products, unlike more marketplace-driven competitors, because
JD has control over its network. Its network was at full capacity even
during the peak days of the pandemic, while other ecommerce platforms could not fulfill orders.

The trend toward more online grocery ordering should continue.
A Forrester survey conducted in April 2020 suggests that the majority of consumers over the age of 65 will do more online shopping in
the future.[89]

JD.com's Birthday Celebration Event: 618

JD.com's anniversary is June 18, 1998, when Liu built a retail booth in a Beijing mall. In honor of that anniversary, in 2005, JD began the shopping festival called 618, which offers significant deals late at night for loyal customers. As with Singles' Day, many customers would postpone their usual shopping routines to take advantage of the discounts. In 2011, JD extended the 618 promotion from one day to a monthlong celebration, and soon other competitors joined the festivities and offered their own discounts. The shopping experience involves omnichannel experiences, including livestreaming.

In the 618 event in June 2020, following the COVID-19-inspired shutdowns, both Alibaba and JD.com saw record numbers of sales, perhaps signaling a recovery with the Chinese consumer. JD.com reported transaction volume that totaled $37.99 billion.[90] This was more than the volume sold the year before for the same festival.

PDD Offers the Best Low-Price Value and Unique Shopping Experience

PDD was launched in 2015 by Colin Huang, an ex-Google employee and serial entrepreneur. Huang's previous experience included working with an operating company to open stores on Alibaba and founding a gaming company. Huang recognized a unique opportunity in China's ecommerce scene.

Over 90% of the payment process in ecommerce was controlled by two independent payment ecosystems: Alibaba's Alipay and Tencent's WeChat. Alipay was tied to Alibaba's marketplaces, Taobao and Tmall. Although WeChat had a relationship with JD, very few transactions were being made directly on the app because it was not tied to a specific marketplace. Building on prior experience, Huang created PDD as a marketplace tied to WeChat and used principles of gamification as the marketing ploy to rapidly acquire new customers. PDD's user base went from zero to 100 million in its first year, then to 200 million in its second year. By year three, PDD had acquired 300 million consumers and GMV (gross merchandise volumes) of over 140 million yuan (US$20.5 billion).[91]

PDD is a marketplace platform, which from day one offered the lowest-priced products; both JD and Tmall have higher prices. Initially, PDD carried products more like what you might see at a dollar store: low-end commodity-type products at rock-bottom prices.

As of May 2020, PDD was China's second most valuable online retailer by market capitalization (although it is still not profitable) and third in actual market share. Given PDD's low prices and low margins, its revenue model is not the same as that of JD.com and Tmall, which each take a cut of transactions made on their platforms. Instead, PDD's revenue stream comes from advertising (special placement on the site or recommendation platform, featuring a box around the offering, or banner ads). In addition, most of PDD's growth comes from the approximately 1 billion Chinese living in small cities and rural areas who are much more price sensitive.[92] At least two-thirds of PDD's customers came from outside the areas of typical ecommerce shoppers at the time.

PDD's Team Pricing Model
PDD initiated the creative innovation of the team pricing model. The basic idea is that for each product consumers want to purchase: (1) if they promote the reference to their friends and family on social networks within WeChat (Pin = together), (2) then they would all get a "team" price that was significantly lower (duo = more savings), and (3) the more they interacted with each other, the more opportunity there was for playing games or for social interaction (duo = more fun). The customer has 24 hours to put together the required number of customers for a specific team to get the reduced price.

While initially customers had to form their own teams, over time they could join teams of strangers. If the team does not solidify, consumers could buy the product themselves, but the individual price was higher. Teams can be as small as 2 people, a tweak from the original 10 people to encourage rapid growth. Now the merchant can set the team size, from 2 to 10.

Using this model, customer acquisition costs are low, far lower than those of competitors. With PDD, like Amazon Prime, the consumer never worries about delivery costs: free shipping is standard. PDD has same-day delivery for fresh products and for some locales; otherwise, delivery times range between 3 and 10 days. (Comparatively, JD's delivery time is much better: one to three days.) Unlike JD, PDD is 100% marketplace; there is no first-party inventory. PDD uses algorithms to personalize offerings, and its pages resemble virtual bazaars where users can scroll and explore different products. All traffic comes from mobile.

This team pricing model is a self-reinforcing virtuous cycle. Each user brings in more people, and the more they bring in, the more they all spend and save, which provides more value for their money. By leveraging existing buyers' networks on WeChat, PDD lowers the costs of acquisition, and its model aligns customers' incentives with its own incentives.

Since there is an incentive to buy the same things at the same time, product and supply chain costs are lower, providing more cost savings. This incentive for synchronous purchase timing leads to better inventory planning and management and better product design to fit consumers' desires. Each of these factors lowers products' costs and allows for better quality. The success of PDD and its team pricing model has spawned imitation. JD.com has launched Jingxi, which is also a group-buying service and operates as a separate app.

More Interaction Among Users Provides Better User Experience and Trust

The more teammates each consumer brings, the more interaction results. This synergy has two advantages. First, it provides a better user experience and fosters more trust. It is also more fun. Keeping the network of friends active helps reactivate buyers through friends' recommendations. Friends discover new opportunities, and they are motivated to share those with their network, keeping buyer engagement high and translating into better retention. This gives PDD a leadership position in the Experiential quadrant.

Second, the social-relational part of the model provides a better understanding of its users. PDD's algorithms can use all the information, each user's behavior, *and* interaction between the users to better serve customers. Friends bring in friends, so information about one person in a network provides good "guesses" about their likely similar friends. Since many purchase decisions are in product categories where consumers do not have strong preferences, people are easily influenced by personal recommendations and can be persuaded to buy at the same time.

Gamification Elements Add Fun to the Shopping Experience

The last piece of the model comes via gamification aspects, which increase the pleasure in the customer experience and create "stickiness." In-app games and promotions are specifically designed to encourage interaction and sharing on the platform using "gaming" principles like streaks. These are supported by sophisticated AI infrastructure that allows for personalized and customized experiences.

One of PDD's more famous gaming applications involves virtual fruit growing on a tree. Users are incentivized to water the tree daily, which helps it grow. They are also incentivized to bring in friends and to not "miss a day." Users collect rewards and cards from purchasing to receive extra benefits. When the virtual tree grows to a certain size, it delivers an actual fruit to the consumer. The choice of which actual products to send is done selectively and based on categories where there are oversupplies.

While Alibaba maximizes the treasure hunt experience, the PDD experience is more like friends' recommendations. Time spent on the app is more browsing-based than search-based. And since 100% of activity is on mobile, PDD is able to capitalize on specific customer behaviors.

Conclusion

For many reasons, Chinese retailing has developed differently from retailing in the United States. To one of my initial points in this chapter about collectivism versus individualism, Chinese internet users are more than three times as likely as US internet users to post online feedback on purchases at least once a month.

Second, the Chinese social media and social commerce landscape is more advanced than in the United States. China is a pioneer in mobile commerce, which accounts for three-quarters of the volume in ecommerce. The infrastructure has evolved to suit these preferences. In China, "super apps" like Alibaba's Alipay or Tencent's WeChat make it easy for consumers to do whatever they want through one app. This not only facilitates easy shopping and payment but encourages social media conversation about purchases.

The link between shopping and entertainment is stronger in China. The ecosystem has developed to serve these preferences. Unlike Amazon, where the goal is convenience and one-click shopping, both Alibaba as a treasure hunt and PDD as a place where friends meet to make recommendations are sites that consumers go to for discovery. Entertainment also comes through shopping, or shoppertainment, and the growth in the market power of KOLs has illustrated that. Singles' Day and other shopping festivals have helped popularize the use of livestreaming as a shopping and entertainment venue.

The physical retail landscape in China has also developed quite differently from that in the United States. US mall growth started in the 1950s and has evolved over the last 70 years. This has resulted in the United States being "over-stored," and long-term leases make it quite difficult for retailers to pivot to respond to changing trends. In China, there is no legacy physical retailing network to unwind. China has been an open economy only since 1992. The lack of physical retailing encouraged fast internet growth, encouraged companies to build the best payment systems to facilitate shopping at lower costs, and helped accelerate solving the complex logistical issues of omnichannel retailing.

China is ahead of the United States in implementing Alibaba's concept of "new retail," or what JD.com calls "borderless retail." Alibaba's Hema stores and JD.com's 7Fresh stores allow for customer-centric omnichannel retailing in a way not seen in the United States.

The Chinese government itself has facilitated the rapid growth of ecommerce business through new policies and tax breaks on retail, informatization, IT, and IoT. Lack of enforcement in sales tax and income tax lowers the cost of ecommerce entrepreneurs on Taobao, creating taxation gray areas. Low labor costs in China help facilitate growth and drive down the picking and packing costs, transit costs, and last-mile delivery costs. In addition, broadband and mobile internet is relatively cheap and available in more rural areas.

Finally, the COVID-19 crisis in 2020 has accelerated the trends that deliver to these Chinese advantages. Given the health crises and the necessity for self-quarantining, the penetration, frequency, and basket size in ecommerce purchasing have been accelerated. In addition, the prioritization in purchasing of essential retail has further strengthened the "new retail" development since most of that innovation was actualized through the grocery channel.

These trends and infrastructure advantages have led to incredible innovation in the Chinese ecommerce market. From the brand development used in the on-site flagship storefronts on Alibaba's Tmall site, to the sense of discovery facilitated by the algorithm-based treasure hunt experience on Taobao, to the logistics expertise and automation leadership pioneered by JD, and finally to the innovation in rapid customer acquisition and the gamification of the shopping experience created by PDD, China has reinvented retail and provided many lessons for the rest of the world.

Conclusion

The retailing industry is fundamentally changing. Most directly, COVID-19 has been the biggest disruptor in the industry, accelerating the trend to ecommerce shopping. But even before that, retailing was in the process of a major transformation amid Amazon's dominance, pervasive use of the mobile phone that provided 24-hour interconnectivity between offline and online communities, and changing shopping patterns exemplified by the digitally native Gen Z and millennial consumers.

In response to these fundamental changes, innovative startups are developing new retail models. These include subscription models, using brick-and-mortar retail stores as showrooms rather than selling spaces, shoppertainment, and new renting and sharing paradigms. In addition to all of this industry disruption, other macro trends include significant technological advances for in-store and online retailing, such as the use of AR and VR and contactless payment; the advent of big data powered by AI; and a reaction to the Great Recession and COVID-19 that has made consumers more price sensitive.

Kahn Retailing Success Matrix

The purpose of this book is to share a framework, the Kahn Retailing Success Matrix, to help make sense of all these changes. The Kahn Retailing Success Matrix allows for the systematic mapping of various retailing strategies on the same axes so they can be compared easily. This provides a common vocabulary for discussing different successful strategic alternatives. It also allows for measurement on the underlying axes over time and provides a graphing tool such that progress can be measured.

Strategically, the framework has several important prescriptions:

1. *It is critical to be the best at one leadership value and then leverage that leadership value to be the best at something else.* It is not OK to be "good enough" at lots of things. In very competitive industries, like that of retailing, it is first necessary to become the best at one of the quadrant strategies, and then leverage that leadership advantage to become the best at a second leadership value. I call this the Two-Quadrant Winning Strategy. Trying to be "the best" at too many things results in suboptimality, so it is necessary to focus on and maintain leadership in two core strengths, and not try to be good at everything. Losing that focus and letting your leadership strengths get diluted is disastrous.

2. *You have to meet fair value on everything where you aren't the best.* The implication here is that while retailers do need to meet customers' minimal expectations on aspects that do not deliver to their strengths, they do not have to be the market leaders in those areas; however, they cannot be subpar either.

3. *Customers' fair-value expectations are constantly increasing as the market gets more competitive.* While retailers only need to be at fair value for activities that are not their strengths, these fair-value goals are moving targets. Smart competitors, like Amazon, are constantly raising the table stakes.

Shopping Is a Customer-centric Omnichannel Experience

The shopping revolution is not about the movement from physical stores to online shopping. Rather, consumers now expect seamless integration across *all* channels. The data from the offline, mobile, and online experiences have to be merged, and progressive retailers must use that comprehensive data to individualize their real-time store experiences. Shoppers expect to be able to search online and pick up in the stores, or search in the store and buy online. This is the new "normal."

Metrics Need to Change

In this new world of retailing, standard metrics like sales per square foot, profit/loss by channel, traffic count, and basket size are not the only metrics to consider—and may not even be the most appropriate. Home Depot executives, for example, are considering new metrics, such as impact to brand impression, digital purchase intent, and customer convenience and experience measures. And as COVID-19 has accelerated consumers' desire for convenience through ecommerce and "buy online, pick up in the store" accessibility, measures like order-to-delivery time, clicks per item, or text analytics become important.

And it is not just metrics in the store. We are moving to more of a platform model, where consumers can transact whenever they want across several channels: physical store, mobile, online, social media, or the IoT. This means that retailers should strive to have ownership of the customer experience across as many channels and functions as possible, and many are failing to measure this.

Kurt Salmon consultants label this omission as the "digital experience gap." They argue one important metric to consider is "share of home," or share of the home ecosystem (e.g., Amazon's Alexa or Apple's Siri).

Here, the retailer that can ultimately control the shopping list has a real advantage. If a consumer is recording all of his or her household needs with Alexa on Amazon Echo, then Amazon is in the driver's seat. Another goal is to increase the frequency of interaction with the consumer so that more data can be collected and mined to better understand what customers want and need. This desire for more interaction with the customer has motivated savvy retailers like Amazon to get into other businesses, such as media, entertainment products, or home services.

Can Traditional Retailers Rebound?

One of the implications of the Kahn Retailing Success Matrix is that retailers that do not lead in two quadrants are susceptible to falling retail sales. We are certainly seeing this play out, as traditional retailers such as Macy's, Sears, and Gap close hundreds of stores and are being forced to continually discount slow-moving inventory. As J.Crew's ex-CEO Mickey Drexler, once lauded as the "merchant prince," said about his core customer: "She's loyal as hell until we go wrong. Then she wants it on sale."

The traditional retailers are "stuck in the middle." Not only are they not the leaders, but traditional retailers have failed to meet the ever-increasing customer expectations that are set by their more progressive competitors.

Traditional retailers are failing in all four quadrants. Amazon and other online retailers have captured sales from customers who now demand the convenience of online shopping and speedy delivery. Sephora and Ulta are luring away the cosmetic and beauty shoppers who crave more interactive and social in-store environments. Vertical fashion brands are shying away from selling their goods through the traditional department store and retailing platforms and are selling their branded products directly to the end user. Finally, the price-sensitive and bargain-loving shoppers are attracted to the everyday low-price treasure hunt experiences of the off-price retailers.

Can the traditional retailers come back? It's possible. Their dreary store experiences have to be updated. They have to get to the state of the art in ecommerce. But that's not enough. They then have to give customers a reason to come to them; they have to find their own leadership strategies.

Probably the best bet for these mainstream retailers is for them to win once again in the Branded Product quadrant and open new channels to compete in the Low Price quadrant. Macy's new CEO has promised that Macy's will be the new "fashion authority." If he can deliver on that promise, that could bring its loyal shoppers back. Macy's has also opened its own off-price treasure hunt experience with its new Backstage stores. Again, if it can move to a leadership strategy here, it could be a viable player.

Similarly, Gap is closing many Gap and Banana Republic stores, which are often "stuck in the middle" with no real leadership positioning. It is reinvesting in Old Navy, which competes effectively in the Low Price quadrant with trending fashion, and in Athleta, which offers a branded product that appeals to a targeted segment. To stay current, these chains will have to adopt some of the strategies of their "fast fashion" competitors and move to fast and flexible supply chains so they can better deliver on fast-moving trends as they are happening.

These are certainly steps in the right direction, but the key question is: Can they succeed and become the leaders they once were, or will it be too little, too late?

Notes

1 Walter Loeb, "More Than 14,500 Stores Are Closing in 2020 So Far—a Number That Will Surely Rise," *Forbes*, July 6, 2020, https://www.forbes.com/sites /walterloeb/2020/07/06/9274-stores-are-closing-in-2020--its-the-pandemic-and -high-debt--more-will-close/?sh=6606fc1d729f; Felix Richter, "Retailers Face Mass Extinction in Pandemic Fallout," Statista, August 24, 2020, https://www .statista.com/chart/22672/number-of-retail-store-closures-in-the-united-states/.

2 Annie Palmer, "Amazon Sales Soar as Pandemic Fuels Online Shopping," CNBC, July 30, 2020, https://www.cnbc.com/2020/07/30/amazon-amzn -earnings-q2-2020.html.

3 Taylor Soper, "Online Grocery Apps Are Thriving During the Covid-19 Crisis. Are They Here to Stay?," *dot.LA*, April 8, 2020, https://dot.la/online-grocery-apps -are-thriving-during-the-covid-19-crisis-are-they-here-to-stay-2645673118.html.

4 Christopher Donnelly and Renato Scaff, "Who Are the Millennial Shoppers? And What Do They Really Want?," Accenture, last accessed December 2020, https://www.accenture.com/us-en/insight-outlook-who-are-millennial-shoppers -what-do-they-really-want-retail.

5 Kurt Salmon, "Navigating the Digital Experience Paradox," September 26, 2016, http://www.kurtsalmon.com/en-us/Retail/vertical-insight/1626/Navigating-the -Digital-Experience-Paradox (page no longer available).

6 Walter Loeb, "Macy's and Other Retailers Need Merchants Who Will Step Out to Win," *Forbes*, July 6, 2017, https://www.forbes.com/sites/walterloeb/2017/07 /06/macys-and-every-other-retailer-as-well-needs-merchants-who-will-step-out -to-win/#18530641af36.

7 eMarketer Retail, "Mixed Feelings: How Shoppers Think About Brick-and-Mortar," May 3, 2017, https://retail.emarketer.com/article/mixed-feelings-how -shoppers-think-about-brick-and-mortar/590a4d28ebd400097ccd5f8b (page no longer available).

8 Matt Day and Spencer Soper, "Amazon U.S. Online Market Share Estimate Cut to 38% from 47%," *Bloomberg*, June 13, 2019, https://www.bloomberg.com/news /articles/2019-06-13/emarketer-cuts-estimate-of-amazon-s-u-s-online-market -share.

9 Sebastian Herrera and Merrill Sherman, "Coronavirus Hobbled Amazon: How the Tech Giant Rebounded for Its Best Earnings Ever," *Wall Street Journal*,

August 6, 2020, https://www.wsj.com/articles/coronavirus-hobbled-amazon -then-the-tech-giant-bounced-back-11596708000.

10   Annie Palmer, "Amazon Reports Sales Growth of 37%, Topping Estimates," CNBC, October 29, 2020, https://www.cnbc.com/2020/10/29/amazon-amzn -earnings-q3-2020.html.

11   Dana Mattioli and Aaron Tilley, "Amazon Has Long Ruled the Cloud. Now It Must Fend Off Rivals," *Wall Street Journal*, January 4, 2020, https://www.wsj .com/articles/amazon-has-long-ruled-the-cloud-now-it-must-fend-off-rivals -11578114008.

12   April Berthene, "82% of US Households Have an Amazon Prime Membership," Digital Commerce 360, July 11, 2019, https://www.digitalcommerce360.com /2019/07/11/82-of-us-households-have-a-amazon-prime-membership.

13   Lance Whitney, "Amazon Prime Members Will Renew Despite Price Hike, Survey Finds," CNET, July 23, 2014, https://www.cnet.com/news/amazon-prime -members-will-almost-all-renew-despite-price-increase/.

14   Bret Kinsella, "Amazon Smart Speaker Market Share Falls to 53% in 2019 with Google the Biggest Beneficiary Rising to 31%, Sonos Also Moves Up," Voicebot. ai, April 28, 2020, https://voicebot.ai/2020/04/28/amazon-smart-speaker-market -share-falls-to-53-in-2019-with-google-the-biggest-beneficiary-rising-to-31 -sonos-also-moves-up.

15   Tatiana Walk-Morris, "Smart Speaker Shopping Falls Short of Projections," Retail Dive, February 5, 2020, https://www.retaildive.com/news/smart-speaker -shopping-falls-short-of-projections/571748.

16   Valentina Pop and Sam Schechner, "Amazon to Face Antitrust Charges from EU over Treatment of Third-Party Sellers," *Wall Street Journal*, June 11, 2020, https://www.wsj.com/articles/amazon-to-face-antitrust-charges-from-eu-over -treatment-of-third-party-sellers-11591871818.

17   Dana Mattioli, "Amazon Scooped Up Data from Its Own Sellers to Launch Competing Products," *Wall Street Journal*, April 24, 2020, https://www.wsj.com /articles/amazon-scooped-up-data-from-its-own-sellers-to-launch-competing -products-11587650015.

18   Karen Weise, "Amazon Knows What You Buy. And It's Building a Big Ad Business from It," *New York Times*, January 20, 2019, https://www.nytimes.com /2019/01/20/technology/amazon-ads-advertising.html.

19   Matthew Johnston, "Amazon Earnings: What Happened," Investopedia, October 29, 2020, https://www.investopedia.com/amazon-q3-2020-earnings-5083872.

20   Tugba Sabanoglu, "Average Annual Amount Spent on Amazon According to U.S. Amazon Prime and Non-Prime Members as of March 2019," Statista, November 30, 2020, https://www.statista.com/statistics/304938/amazon-prime -and-non-prime-members-average-sales-spend/.

21 Frank Holland, "Amazon Is Delivering Nearly Two-Thirds of Its Own Packages as e-Commerce Continues Pandemic Boom," CNBC, August 13, 2020, https://www.cnbc.com/2020/08/13/amazon-is-delivering-nearly-two-thirds-of-its-own-packages.html.

22 Audrey Schomer, "How Amazon Advertising Is Eating Into the Digital Ad Market Currently Dominated by Google & Facebook in 2020," Business Insider, December 18, 2019, https://www.businessinsider.com/amazon-advertising-market-outlook.

23 David Streitfeld, "What Happens After Amazon's Domination Is Complete? Its Bookstore Offers Clues," New York Times, June 23, 2019, https://www.nytimes.com/2019/06/23/technology/amazon-domination-bookstore-books.html.

24 Streitfeld, "What Happens After Amazon's Domination Is Complete?"

25 Alexandra Berzon, Shane Shifflett, and Justin Scheck, "Amazon Has Ceded Control of Its Site. The Result: Thousands of Banned, Unsafe or Mislabeled Products," Wall Street Journal, August 23, 2019, https://www.wsj.com/articles/amazon-has-ceded-control-of-its-site-the-result-thousands-of-banned-unsafe-or-mislabeled-products-11566564990.

26 Russell Redman, "Amazon Leads in Online Grocery Shopper Satisfaction," Supermarket News, July 10, 2020, https://www.supermarketnews.com/online-retail/amazon-leads-online-grocery-shopper-satisfaction.

27 Redman, "Amazon Leads in Online Grocery Shopper Satisfaction."

28 Lilian Diep, "Amazon and Whole Foods Implement New Strategies, Hire 75K More Team Members," Deli Market News, April 17, 2020, https://www.delimarketnews.com/buyside-news/amazon-and-whole-foods-implement-new-strategies-hire-75k-more-team-members/lilian-diep/tue-04142020-0854/9561.

29 Katie Richards, "How Walmart Plans to Turn Around Its Fashion Business in 2020," Glossy, January 3, 2020, https://www.glossy.co/fashion/how-walmart-plans-to-turn-around-its-fashion-business-in-2020.

30 Sarah Nassauer, "With His TikTok Pursuit, Walmart CEO Seeks to Revamp Retailer Again," Wall Street Journal, August 28, 2020, https://www.wsj.com/articles/with-his-tiktok-pursuit-walmart-ceo-seeks-to-revamp-retailer-again-11598637043.

31 Daphne Howland, "Why Walmart Is Betting Big on E-Commerce Acquisitions," Retail Dive, May 31, 2017, https://www.retaildive.com/news/why-wal-mart-is-betting-big-on-e-commerce-acquisitions/443177/.

32 Shelley E. Kohan, "If You Can't Join Them, Buy Them!," Robin Report, September 2, 2020, https://www.therobinreport.com/if-you-cant-join-them-buy-them/.

33 Dan Ochwat, "Walmart's Great Value Brand Earns More Than $27 Billion Annually," Store Brands, February 18, 2020, https://storebrands.com/walmarts-great-value-brand-earns-more-27-billion-annually.

34   Robin Lewis, "Shopify Who? Ask Walmart," Robin Report, June 28, 2020, https://www.therobinreport.com/shopify-who-ask-walmart/.

35   Emily Mondloch, "It's a New Day for Dollar Stores," Baber Martin Agency, September 15, 2017, https://www.barbermartin.com/dollar-stores-retail -expansion/ (page no longer available).

36   Melissa Repko, "Target Aims to Make Its Booming Online Business More Profitable with New Technology, Small Sort Centers," CNBC, May 20, 2020, https://www.cnbc.com/2020/05/20/heres-how-target-aims-to-make-its-booming -online-business-more-profitable.html.

37   Kavita Kumar, "Target Going Ahead with Special Limited-Edition Designer Partnership on Dresses," Star Tribune, May 19, 2020, https://www.startribune .com/target-going-ahead-with-special-limited-edition-designer-partnership-on -dresses/570556682/.

38   Rebecca San Juan, "Get Your Grocery Bags Ready: Aldi Is Adding Three South Florida Locations This Fall," Miami Herald, September 2, 2020, https://www .miamiherald.com/news/business/real-estate-news/article245410115.html.

39   Kantar, "Totaling $3.81 Trillion in Value, the BrandZ Top 100 US Brands Are Worth More Than the GDP of Germany, the Fourth Largest Economy in the World," Cision PR Newswire, November 14, 2019, https://www.prnewswire.com /news-releases/totaling-3-81-trillion-in-value-the-brandz-top-100-us-brands -are-worth-more-than-the-gdp-of-germany-the-fourth-largest-economy-in-the -world-300957486.html.

40   Jenn Wohletz, "Top Five Reasons Why People Love Trader Joe's So F*@%ing Much," Westword, February 17, 2012, http://www.westword.com/restaurants /top-five-reasons-why-people-love-trader-joes-so-f-ing-much-5773473.

41   Andy Dunn, "The Book of DNVB: The Rise of Digitally Native Vertical Brands," Medium, May 9, 2016, https://medium.com/@dunn/digitally-native-vertical -brands-b26a26f2cf83.

42   Emma Bowman and Sarah McCammon, "Can Fast Fashion and Sustainability Be Stitched Together?," NPR, July 27, 2019, https://www.npr.org/2019/07/27 /745418569/can-fast-fashion-and-sustainability-be-stitched-together.

43   Jamie Grill-Goodman, "Zara Parent to Close 1,200 Stores and Invest $3 Billion in E-Commerce," RIS News, June 10, 2020, https://risnews.com/zara-parent -close-1200-stores-and-invest-3-billion-e-commerce.

44   Angela Self, "Getting the Inside Scoop on Mattress Pricing," Globe and Mail, June 2, 2011, https://www.theglobeandmail.com/globe-investor/personal -finance/getting-the-inside-scoop-on-mattress-pricing/article581813/.

45   Caroline Jansen, "Casper Expands Physical Presence Through Tie-up with Sam's Club," Retail Dive, August 10, 2020, https://www.retaildive.com /news/casper-expands-physical-presence-through-tie-up-with-sams-club /583220.

46 Interbrand, "Best Global Brands 2019," Ranking the Brands, last accessed December 2020, https://www.rankingthebrands.com/The-Brand-Rankings.aspx ?rankingID=37&year=1273.

47 Interbrand, *A New Decade of Possibility: Best Global Brands 2020* (report), 2020, https://learn.interbrand.com/hubfs/INTERBRAND/Interbrand_Best_Global _Brands%202020.pdf.

48 J. N. Kapferer, *Kapferer on Luxury: How Luxury Brands Can Grow yet Remain Rare* (Philadelphia: Kogan Page, 2015).

49 Tamison O'Connor, "Selling Fashion to the 1% During a Pandemic," Business of Fashion, August 4, 2020, https://www.businessoffashion.com/articles /professional/selling-fashion-to-the-1-during-a-pandemic.

50 BOF Team, "The BoF Podcast: Neiman Marcus Chief Executive Sees Stores as Vital for Digital Growth," Business of Fashion, July 16, 2020, https://www .businessoffashion.com/articles/podcasts/the-bof-podcast-neiman-marcus-chief -executive-sees-stores-as-vital-for-digital-growth.

51 Zoe Suen, "How the Wholesale Crisis Could Benefit Independent Fashion Brands," Business of Fashion, July 10, 2020, https://www.businessoffashion.com /articles/professional/wholesale-crisis-could-benefit-independent-fashion -brands-galeries-lafayette-burberry-selfridges.

52 Greg Grigorian, "Luxury Brands Are Digitizing, and China Is Their Fiercest Digitizer," Pandaily, December 17, 2019, https://pandaily.com/luxury-brands-are -digitizing-and-china-is-their-fiercest-digitizer.

53 Daphne Howland, "The Comeback of the Brick-and-Mortar Store," Retail Dive, January 13, 2020, https://www.retaildive.com/news/the-comeback-of-the-brick -and-mortar-store/570290/.

54 Suzy Menkes, "Retail Is Broken: Angela Ahrendts Has a Plan," Vogue Business, January 28, 2019, https://www.voguebusiness.com/companies/angela-ahrendts -apple-retail-strategy.

55 Ruth La Ferla, "The Cult of the Line: It's Not About the Merch," *New York Times*, August 3, 2017, https://www.nytimes.com/2017/08/03/fashion/waiting-in-line -supreme-streetwear-merch.html.

56 Roberto Fontana, Stéphan J. G. Girod, and Martin Králik, "How Luxury Brands Can Beat Counterfeiters," *Harvard Business Review*, May 24, 2019, https://hbr .org/2019/05/how-luxury-brands-can-beat-counterfeiters.

57 Vikram Alexei Kansara, "Amid Pandemic, Luxury Leaders Seize Digital Opportunity to Gain on Rivals," Business of Fashion, July 31, 2020, https://www .businessoffashion.com/articles/professional/luxury-coronavirus-digital-lvmh -kering-prada-q2-2020-results.

58 Chantal Fernandez, "Farfetch Sales Soared During Lockdowns," Business of Fashion, August 14, 2020, https://www.businessoffashion.com/articles /professional/farfetch-results-q2-2020-coronavirus-luxury-fashion-ecommerce.

59   Evie Liu, "There's One 'Unquestioned' Leader in Grocery Prices," *Barron's*,
     October 13, 2017, https://www.barrons.com/articles/theres-one-unquestioned
     -leader-in-grocery-prices-1507927977.

60   Angel Gonzalez and Janet I. Tu, "Is Amazon a Threat to Costco? Survey Weighs
     Coexistence," *Seattle Times*, October 26, 2016, https://www.seattletimes.com
     /business/amazon/rivals-amazon-costco-can-both-thrive-survey-says/.

61   Valuewalk, "Costco Wholesale: A Standout in the Saturated Retail Sector,"
     Yahoo! Finance, March 30, 2020, https://finance.yahoo.com/news/costco
     -wholesale-standout-saturated-retail-190957105.html.

62   Walter Loeb, "Costco Looks for the New Normal After First COVID-19 Wave,"
     Forbes, May 29, 2020, https://www.forbes.com/sites/walterloeb/2020/05/29
     /costco-looks-for-the-new-normal-after-first-covid-19-wave/.

63   Rob Walker, "Why TJ Maxx Doesn't Need E-Commerce to Survive the
     Pandemic," Marker, August 6, 2020, https://marker.medium.com/why-tj-maxx
     -doesnt-need-e-commerce-to-survive-the-pandemic-2b9cb766cedc?gi=sd.

64   Walker, "Why TJ Maxx Doesn't Need E-Commerce."

65   Emily Gerstell, Sophie Marchessou, Jennifer Schmidt, and Emma Spagnuolo,
     "How COVID-19 Is Changing the World of Beauty," McKinsey & Company,
     May 8, 2020, https://www.mckinsey.com/industries/consumer-packaged-goods
     /our-insights/how-covid-19-is-changing-the-world-of-beauty.

66   Rita Liao, "Pinduoduo Cements Position as China's Second-Largest Ecommerce
     Player," TechCrunch, June 27, 2019, https://techcrunch.com/2019/06/26
     /pinduoduo-second-biggest-china-ecommerce/.

67   Chris Biggs, Ameé Chande, Erica Matthews, Pierre Mercier, Angela Wang, and
     Linda Zou, "What China Reveals About the Future of Shopping," BCG, May 4,
     2017, https://www.bcg.com/en-us/publications/2017/retail-globalization-china
     -reveals-future-shopping.

68   John Ninia, "The United States Lags Behind China in Adopting Mobile
     Payments: BusinessFeed," Cornell SC Johnson, October 23, 2019, https://
     business.cornell.edu/hub/2019/10/23/united-states-china-mobile-payments/.

69   Ruchi Gupta, "Just How Far Ahead Is Alibaba in China's e-Commerce Market?,"
     Market Realist, July 17, 2019, https://marketrealist.com/2019/07/just-how-far
     -ahead-is-alibaba-in-chinas-e-commerce-market/.

70   Pete Stein, "What US Marketers Can Learn from Social Commerce in China,"
     Forbes, August 7, 2014, https://www.forbes.com/sites/onmarketing/2014/08/07
     /what-us-marketers-can-learn-from-social-commerce-in-china/.

71   Daniel Keyes and Greg Magana, "Chinese Fintechs Like Ant Financial's Alipay
     and Tencent's WeChat Are Rapidly Growing Their Financial Services Ecosystems,"
     Business Insider, December 18, 2019, https://www.businessinsider.com/china
     -fintech-alipay-wechat.

72 "eMarketer Projects Surge in Mobile Payments in China," eMarketer, November 2, 2017, https://www.emarketer.com/Article/eMarketer-Projects -Surge-Mobile-Payments-China/1016695.

73 Wei Wei, "BAT+头条占据七成移动互联网使用时长_用户," Sohu, April 24, 2019, https://www.sohu.com/a/310012220_115865.

74 Alizila Staff, "What China Reveals About the Future of Shopping," Alizila, May 4, 2017, https://www.alizila.com/china-reveals-future-shopping/.

75 Bloomberg News, "Tencent-Backed Little Red Book Seeks $6 Billion Valuation," *Bloomberg*, January 10, 2020, https://www.bloomberg.com/news/articles/2020 -01-10/tencent-backed-little-red-book-said-to-seek-6-billion-valuation.

76 Sergei Klebnikov, "Alibaba's 11/11 Singles' Day by the Numbers: A Record $38 Billion Haul," *Forbes*, November 11, 2019, https://www.forbes.com/sites /sergeiklebnikov/2019/11/11/alibabas-1111-singles-day-by-the-numbers-a-record -38-billion-haul/.

77 Ruonan Zheng, "Livestream Goldmine: Kim Kardashian Meets Chinese Top Livestreamer Viya," Jing Daily, November 10, 2019, https://jingdaily.com /livesteam-goldmine-kim-kardashian-meets-chinese-top-livestreamer-viya/.

78 Yihan Ma, "Leading B2C Retailers' Share of Sales in Total Retail e-Commerce Sales in China in 2019," Statista, July 22, 2020, https://www.statista.com /statistics/880212/sales-share-of-the-leading-e-commerce-retailers-in-china/.

79 Ma, "Leading B2C Retailers' Share of Sales."

80 Ruchi Gupta, "Just How Far Ahead Is Alibaba in China's e-Commerce Market?," Market Realist, July 17, 2019, https://marketrealist.com/2019/07/just-how-far -ahead-is-alibaba-in-chinas-e-commerce-market/.

81 Manish Singh, "Alibaba to Invest $3.3B to Bump Its Stake in Logistics Unit Cainiao," TechCrunch, November 8, 2019, https://techcrunch.com/2019/11/08 /alibaba-cainiao-63-percent/.

82 Singh, "Alibaba to Invest $3.3B."

83 Jack Ma, "'Unparalleled Ruthlessness' Awaits: Jack Ma's Letter to Alibaba Employees," *Wall Street Journal*, May 7, 2014, https://www.wsj.com/articles/BL -CJB-21993.

84 Marc Bain, "The Unique Challenges of Selling Fashion in China," Quartz, January 15, 2020, https://qz.com/1785406/allbirds-and-tmall-on-the-challenges -of-selling-fashion-in-china/.

85 Lan Luan, Aimee Kim, Daniel Zipser, Minyi Su, Adrian Lo, Cherry Chen, and Cherie Zhang, *China Luxury Report 2019*, 2019, https://www.mckinsey.com /~/media/mckinsey/featured%20insights/china/how%20young%20chinese %20consumers%20are%20reshaping%20global%20luxury/mckinsey-china -luxury-report-2019-how-young-chinese-consumers-are-reshaping-global -luxury.ashx.

86 Jules Scully, "Unilever Partners with JD.com to Expand Its Reach in China," FoodBev Media, August 16, 2018, https://www.foodbev.com/news/unilever-partners-with-jd-com-to-expand-its-reach-in-china.

87 JD.com, "JD.com Speeds Package Deliveries with New Parcel Delivery Service for Chinese Consumers," PR Newswire, October 25, 2018, https://www.prnewswire.com/news-releases/jdcom-speeds-package-deliveries-with-new-parcel-delivery-service-for-chinese-consumers-300738254.html.

88 Stefan Van Rompaey, "Say Hello to 7Fresh, JD.com's High-Tech Supermarket," RetailDetail, April 1, 2020, https://www.retaildetail.eu/en/news/food/say-hello-7fresh-jdcoms-high-tech-supermarket.

89 Satish Meena and Ziaofeng Wang, "China Shopper Insights and the Impact of Covid-19," Forrester, May 29, 2020, https://www.forrester.com/report/China+Shopper+Insights+And+The+Impact+Of+COVID19/-/E-RES160758.

90 Arjun Kharpal, "Alibaba and JD.com Handle a Record $136.51 Billion in Sales During Major Chinese Shopping Event," CNBC, June 19, 2020, https://www.cnbc.com/2020/06/19/alibaba-jdcom-handle-record-sales-during-618-event.html.

91 Kharpal, "Alibaba and JD.com Handle a Record $136.51 Billion in Sales."

92 Winter Nie and Yunfei Feng, "Pinduoduo, China's Social e-Commerce Company, Is at a Crossroads," IMD Business School, February 4, 2019, https://www.imd.org/research-knowledge/articles/pdd-ecommerce-for-the-underserved/.

Bibliography

Introduction

Andrews, Travis M. "America Is 'Over-Stored' and Payless ShoeSource Is the Latest Victim." *Washington Post*, April 5, 2017. https://www.washingtonpost.com/news/morning-mix/wp/2017/04/05/america-is-over-stored-and-payless-shoesource-is-the-latest-victim/.

BI Intelligence. "Amazon Accounts for 43% of US Online Retail Sales." Business Insider, February 3, 2017. http://www.businessinsider.com/amazon-accounts-for-43-of-us-online-retail-sales-2017-2.

Chitrakorn, Kati. "5 Technologies Transforming Retail in 2018." Business of Fashion, January 19, 2018. https://www.businessoffashion.com/articles/fashion-tech/5-technologies-transforming-retail.

Clark, Patrick, and Dorothy Gambrell. "These Cities Have Too Many Stores, and They're Still Building." *Bloomberg*, June 12, 2017. https://www.bloomberg.com/news/articles/2017-06-12/what-s-killing-american-retail-take-a-look-at-this-chart-for-a-start.

Donnelly, Christopher, and Renato Scaff. "Who Are the Millennial Shoppers? And What Do They Really Want?" Accenture. Last accessed December 2020. https://www.accenture.com/us-en/insight-outlook-who-are-millennial-shoppers-what-do-they-really-want-retail.

Farner, Shawn. "How Big Data Is Changing the Retail Industry." Disruptor Daily, November 10, 2017. https://www.disruptordaily.com/big-data-changing-retail-industry/.

Green, Dennis, and Megan Harney. "More Than 8,000 Store Closures Were Announced in 2017—Here's the Full List." Business Insider, December 20, 2017. http://www.businessinsider.com/stores-closures-announced-in-2017-2017-12/#radioshack-1430-stores-1.

Howard, Robert, Jack Horst, Michele Orndorff, and Paul Schottmiller. "Surviving the Brave New World of Food Retailing: A Roadmap to Relevance for the Future for Food Retailers." Kurt Salmon/Coca Cola Retailing Research Council, 2016. https://www.ccrrc.org/2017/01/26/surviving-brave-new-world-food-retailing-roadmap-relevance-future.

Hyken, Shep. "Sixty-Four Percent of U.S. Households Have Amazon Prime." *Forbes*, June 17, 2017. https://www.forbes.com/sites/shephyken/2017/06/17/sixty-four-percent-of-u-s-households-have-amazon-prime/#6b2f48784586.

Kline, Daniel B. "More Than 15,000 Stores Could Close Permanently in 2020." Motley Fool, March 28, 2020. https://www.fool.com/investing/2020/03/28/more-than -15000-stores-close-permanently-2020.aspx.

Loeb, Walter. "More Than 14,500 Stores Are Closing in 2020 So Far—a Number That Will Surely Rise." *Forbes*, July 6, 2020. https://www.forbes.com/sites/walterloeb/2020 /07/06/9274-stores-are-closing-in-2020--its-the-pandemic-and-high-debt--more-will -close/?sh=6606fc1d729f.

Medal, Andrew. "4 Things You Need to Know About Gen Z's Shopping Habits." *Inc.*, November 27, 2017. https://www.inc.com/andrew-medal/how-to-give-gen-z-ers -shopping-experience-they-want.html.

Palmer, Annie. "Amazon Sales Soar as Pandemic Fuels Online Shopping." CNBC, July 30, 2020. https://www.cnbc.com/2020/07/30/amazon-amzn-earnings-q2-2020.html.

Pandolph, Stephanie, and Jonathan Camhi. "Amazon Prime Subscribers Hit 80 Million." Business Insider, April 27, 2017. http://www.businessinsider.com/amazon -prime-subscribers-hit-80-million-2017-4.

Pickard, Katie. "Generation Z and Its 3 Most Important Consumer Behaviors." Precision Dialogue, February 6, 2017. http://www.precisiondialogue.com/generation -z-consumer-behaviors/.

Pinsker, Joe. "Oh No, They've Come Up with Another Generation Label." *Atlantic*, February 21, 2020. https://www.theatlantic.com/family/archive/2020/02/generation -after-gen-z-named-alpha/606862/.

Reda, Susan. "21 Ways Amazon Changed the Face of Retail." *Stores Magazine*, September 2016, pp. 30–33.

Rey, Jason Del. "Amazon Was Already Powerful: The Coronavirus Pandemic Cleared the Way to Dominance." *Vox*, April 10, 2020. https://www.vox.com/recode/2020/4/10 /21215953/amazon-fresh-walmart-grocery-delivery-coronavirus-retail-store-closures.

Reynolds, Cormac. "5 Ways Big Data Is Changing Retail and How We Shop and Sell." Data Floq, November 19, 2015. https://datafloq.com/read/5-ways-big-data-changing -retail-shop-sell/1682.

Richter, Felix. "Retailers Face Mass Extinction in Pandemic Fallout." Statista, August 24, 2020. https://www.statista.com/chart/22672/number-of-retail-store-closures-in-the -united-states/.

Salmon, Kurt. "Navigating the Digital Experience Paradox." September 26, 2016. http:// www.kurtsalmon.com/en-us/Retail/vertical-insight/1626/Navigating-the-Digital -Experience-Paradox (page no longer available).

Smiley, Lauren. "Stitch Fix's Radical Data-Driven Way to Sell Clothes—$1.2 Billion Last Year—Is Reinventing Retail." *Fast Company*, February 20, 2019. https://www .fastcompany.com/90298900/stitch-fix-most-innovative-companies-2019.

Sonsev, Veronika. "Retail Technology and Marketing Trends on the Rise for 2018." *Fortune*, January 22, 2018. https://www.forbes.com/sites/veronikasonsev/2018/01/22 /retail-technology-and-marketing-trends-on-the-rise-for-2018/#10b5f7ec64c0.

Soper, Taylor. "Online Grocery Apps Are Thriving During the Covid-19 Crisis. Are They Here to Stay?" *dot.LA*, April 8, 2020. https://dot.la/online-grocery-apps-are -thriving-during-the-covid-19-crisis-are-they-here-to-stay-2645673118.html.

Thomas, Lauren. "Bankruptcies Will Continue to Rock Retail in 2018: Here's What You Need to Watch." CNBC, December 13, 2017. https://www.cnbc.com/2017/12/13 /bankruptcies-will-continue-to-rock-retail-in-2018-watch-these-trends.html.

Thompson, Derek. "What in the World Is Causing the Retail Meltdown of 2017?" *Atlantic*, April 10, 2017. https://www.theatlantic.com/business/archive/2017/04/retail -meltdown-of-2017/522384/.

Treacy, Michael, and Fred Wiersema. *The Discipline of Market Leaders: Choose Your Customers, Narrow Your Focus, Dominate Your Market.* Reading, MA: Addison-Wesley, 1995.

Wertz, Boris. "The Next Big E-Commerce Wave: Vertically Integrated Commerce." TechCrunch, September 29, 2012. https://techcrunch.com/2012/09/29/the-next-big -e-commerce-wave-vertically-integrated-commerce/.

Chapter 1

Day, Matt, and Spencer Soper. "Amazon U.S. Online Market Share Estimate Cut to 38% from 47%." *Bloomberg*, June 13, 2019. https://www.bloomberg.com/news/articles/2019 -06-13/emarketer-cuts-estimate-of-amazon-s-u-s-online-market-share.

eMarketer Retail. "Mixed Feelings: How Shoppers Think About Brick-and-Mortar." May 3, 2017. https://retail.emarketer.com/article/mixed-feelings-how-shoppers-think -about-brick-and-mortar/590a4d28ebd400097ccd5f8b (page no longer available).

Howard, Robert, Jack Horst, Michele Orndorff, and Paul Schottmiller, "Surviving the Brave New World of Food Retailing: A Roadmap to Relevance for the Future for Food Retailers." Kurt Salmon/Coca Cola Retailing Research Council, 2016. https://www .ccrrc.org/2017/01/26/surviving-brave-new-world-food-retailing-roadmap-relevance -future.

Krantz, Matt. "Amazon Just Surpassed Walmart in Market Cap." *USA Today*, July 23, 2015. https://www.usatoday.com/story/money/markets/2015/07/23/amazon-worth-more -walmart/30588783/.

Loeb, Walter. "Macy's and Other Retailers Need Merchants Who Will Step Out to Win." *Forbes*, July 6, 2017. https://www.forbes.com/sites/walterloeb/2017/07/06/macys -and-every-other-retailer-as-well-needs-merchants-who-will-step-out-to-win /#18530641af36.

Ruff, Corinne. "7 Retail Execs Envision the Future of Stores." Retail Dive, February 13, 2018. https://www.retaildive.com/news/7-retail-execs-envision-the-future-of-stores /516795/.

Salmon, Kurt. "Navigating the Digital Experience Paradox." September 26, 2016. http://www.kurtsalmon.com/en-us/Retail/vertical-insight/1626/Navigating-the -Digital-Experience-Paradox.

Treacy, Michael, and Fred Wiersema. *The Discipline of Market Leaders: Choose Your Customers, Narrow Your Focus, Dominate Your Market.* Reading, MA: Addison-Wesley, 1995.

Wahba, Phil. "Amazon Will Make Up 50% of All U.S. E-Commerce by 2021." *Fortune*, April 20, 2017. http://fortune.com/2017/04/10/amazon-retail/.

Chapter 2

Achim, Adina-Laura, and Wenzhuo Wu. "Can Amazon's New Luxury Platform Challenge Alibaba's?" Jing Daily, March 9, 2020. https://jingdaily.com/can-amazons-new-luxury-platform-challenge-alibabas/.

Acosta, Gina. "EXCLUSIVE: Inside Amazon's New Fresh Grocery Banner." Progressive Grocer, August 27, 2020. https://progressivegrocer.com/exclusive-inside-amazons-new-fresh-grocery-banner.

Amazon.com. "Jeff Bezos' 2016 Letter to Shareholders." April 17, 2017. https://www.amazon.com/p/feature/z6o9g6sysxur57t.

———. "Powering Earth's Best Customer Service Experience." Accessed March 30, 2018. https://www.amazon.jobs/en-gb/team/customer-service-technology.

———. "Working at Amazon." Accessed March 30, 2018. https://www.amazon.com/p/feature/cdkk293z8nzm7q8.

Berthene, April. "82% of US Households Have an Amazon Prime Membership." Digital Commerce 360, July 11, 2019. https://www.digitalcommerce360.com/2019/07/11/82-of-us-households-have-a-amazon-prime-membership/.

Berzon, Alexandra, Shane Shifflett, and Justin Scheck. "Amazon Has Ceded Control of Its Site. The Result: Thousands of Banned, Unsafe or Mislabeled Products." *Wall Street Journal*, August 23, 2019. https://www.wsj.com/articles/amazon-has-ceded-control-of-its-site-the-result-thousands-of-banned-unsafe-or-mislabeled-products-11566564990.

Bishop, Todd. "Amazon Forms 'Counterfeit Crimes Unit,' Under Pressure to Escalate Fight Against Fake Products." GeekWire, June 24, 2020. https://www.geekwire.com/2020/amazon-forms-counterfeit-crimes-unit-pressure-escalate-fight-fake-products/.

Bloomberg. "Amazon Wins Business from Reluctant Brands After Coronavirus Closes Stores." Business of Fashion, May 5, 2020. https://www.businessoffashion.com/articles/news-analysis/amazon-wins-business-from-reluctant-brands-after-virus-closes-stores.

Bowman, Jeremy. "Amazon Could Be Your Healthcare Provider Sooner Than You Think." Motley Fool, September 28, 2019. https://www.fool.com/investing/2019/09/28/amazon-could-be-your-healthcare-provider-sooner-th.aspx.

Broida, Rick. "You Just Got Your First Amazon Dash Button, Now What?" CNET, December 8, 2017. https://www.cnet.com/how-to/you-just-got-your-first-amazon-dash-button-now-what/.

CB Insights. "Amazon Strategy Teardown: Building New Business Pillars in AI, Next-Gen Logistics, and Enterprise Cloud Apps." 2017. https://www.cbinsights.com /research/report/amazon-strategy-teardown/.

———. "23 Lessons from Jeff Bezos' Annual Letters to Shareholders." CB Insights Research, July 17, 2020. https://www.cbinsights.com/research/bezos-amazon -shareholder-letters/.

Chafkin, Max. "Amazon Needs to Watch What It Eats." *Bloomberg*, July 31, 2017. https://www.bloomberg.com/news/articles/2017-07-31/amazon-needs-to-watch-what -it-eats.

CNBC. "Amazon's $13.7 Billion Bet on Online Grocery Ordering Hasn't Convinced Shoppers to Stay Home." US Stock Info, October 17, 2017. https://stockinfo.us/2017/10 /17/cnbc-amazon-s-13-7-billion-bet-on-online-grocery-ordering-hasn-t-convinced -shoppers-to-stay-home/.

Conti, Samantha, and *WWD* Staff. "Amazon Said Forging Ahead with Luxury Platform." Yahoo! Finance, August 25, 2020. https://finance.yahoo.com/news/amazon -said-forging-ahead-luxury-040113540.html.

De León, Concepción. "Drone Delivery? Amazon Moves Closer with F.A.A. Approval." *New York Times*, August 31, 2020. https://www.nytimes.com/2020/08/31 /business/amazon-drone-delivery.html.

Diep, Lilian. "Amazon and Whole Foods Implement New Strategies, Hire 75K More Team Members." Deli Market News, April 17, 2020. https://www.delimarketnews .com/buyside-news/amazon-and-whole-foods-implement-new-strategies-hire-75k -more-team-members/lilian-diep/tue-04142020-0854/9561.

Dumaine, Brian. "Amazon Was Built for the Pandemic—and Will Likely Emerge from It Stronger Than Ever." *Fortune*, May 18, 2020. https://fortune.com/2020/05/18 /amazon-business-jeff-bezos-amzn-sales-revenue-coronavirus-pandemic/.

Gabor, Deb. "How the Amazon-Sears Deal Could Make the Smart Home a Reality." *Fortune*, July 26, 2017. http://fortune.com/2017/07/26/amazon-sears-kenmore-smart -home/.

Gasparro, Annie, and Laura Stevens. "Amazon's Grocery Ambitions Spell Trouble for Big Food Brands." *Wall Street Journal*, June 26, 2017. https://www.wsj.com/articles /amazons-grocery-ambitions-spell-trouble-for-big-food-brands-1498469402.

Goel, Vindu. "Amazon, in Hunt for Lower Prices, Recruits Indian Merchants." *New York Times*, November 26, 2017. https://www.nytimes.com/2017/11/26/technology /amazon-india-merchants.html.

Hays, Kali. "Amazon Inks Violet Grey Deal: Sources." *WWD*, July 28, 2017. http:// wwd.com/business-news/financial/amazon-violet-grey-second-quarter-luxury -beauty-10953327/.

Herrera, Sebastian. "Jeff Wilke, Early Amazon Executive and Lieutenant to Jeff Bezos, Plans to Retire." *Wall Street Journal*, August 21, 2020. https://www.wsj.com/articles

/jeff-wilke-amazons-ceo-of-worldwide-consumer-plans-to-retire-11598017252?st
=mclcg74jf33wa6u.

Herrera, Sebastian, and Merrill Sherman. "Coronavirus Hobbled Amazon: How the
Tech Giant Rebounded for Its Best Earnings Ever." *Wall Street Journal*, August 6,
2020. https://www.wsj.com/articles/coronavirus-hobbled-amazon-then-the-tech
-giant-bounced-back-11596708000.

Holland, Frank. "Amazon Is Delivering Nearly Two-Thirds of Its Own Packages as
e-Commerce Continues Pandemic Boom." CNBC, August 13, 2020. https://www.cnbc
.com/2020/08/13/amazon-is-delivering-nearly-two-thirds-of-its-own-packages.html.

Howland, Daphne. "Amazon Smashes Cyber Monday Record." Retail Dive,
November 30, 2017. https://www.retaildive.com/news/amazon-smashes-cyber
-monday-record/511975/.

Jarvey, Natalie. "Amazon's Hollywood Shopping Cart Secrets." *Hollywood Reporter*,
July 15, 2015. https://www.hollywoodreporter.com/features/amazon-prime-day
-hollywood-shopping-808533.

Johnston, Matthew. "Amazon Earnings: What Happened." Investopedia, October 29,
2020. https://www.investopedia.com/amazon-q3-2020-earnings-5083872.

Kim, Eugene. "Amazon Quietly Launched an App Called Relay to Go After Truck
Drivers." CNBC, November 16, 2017. https://www.cnbc.com/2017/11/16/amazon
-quietly-launched-an-app-called-relay-to-go-after-truck-drivers.html.

———. "Amazon Quietly Removes Promotional Spots That Gave Special Treatment to
Its Own Products as Scrutiny of Tech Giants Grows." CNBC, April 3, 2019. https://
www.cnbc.com/2019/04/03/amazon-removes-special-promo-spots-for-private-label
-products.html.

Kim, Tae. "Buy Amazon Because Alexa Will Drive $10 Billion in Sales by 2020, RBC's
Mahaney Predicts." CNBC, December 21, 2017. https://www.cnbc.com/2017/12/21
/buy-amazon-because-alexa-will-drive-10-billion-in-sales-rbc-capital.html.

Kim, W. Chan, Renee Mauborgne, and Oh Young Koo. "Amazon: Successes and
Failures of Amazon's Growth Strategies: Causes and Consequences." Case Study
IN1397-PDF-ENG. *Harvard Business Review*, September 25, 2017. https://hbr.org
/product/successes-and-failures-of-amazons-growth-strategies-causes-and
-consequences/IN1397-PDF-ENG.

Kinsella, Bret. "Amazon Smart Speaker Market Share Falls to 53% in 2019 with
Google the Biggest Beneficiary Rising to 31%, Sonos Also Moves Up." Voicebot.ai,
April 28, 2020. https://voicebot.ai/2020/04/28/amazon-smart-speaker-market-share
-falls-to-53-in-2019-with-google-the-biggest-beneficiary-rising-to-31-sonos-also
-moves-up.

Kirby, Julia, and Thomas A. Stewart. "The Institutional Yes." *Harvard Business
Review*, October 2007. https://hbr.org/2007/10/the-institutional-yes.

Kittilaksanawong, Wiboon, and Auriela Karp. "Amazon Go: Venturing into
Traditional Retail." Case Study W17398-PDF-ENG. *Harvard Business Review*,

June 28, 2017. https://hbr.org/product/amazon-go-venturing-into-traditional-retail/W17398-PDF-ENG.

Lashinsky, Adam. "Amazon's Jeff Bezos: The Ultimate Disrupter." *Fortune*, November 16, 2012. http://fortune.com/2012/11/16/amazons-jeff-bezos-the-ultimate-disrupter/.

Maloney, Greg. "What's in Store for 2018?" *Stores Magazine*, December 4, 2017. https://stores.org/2017/12/04/looking-forward/.

Martinez, Michael. "Amazon: Everything You Wanted to Know About Its Algorithm and Innovation." IEEE Internet Computing, September 27, 2017. https://www.computer.org/internet-computing/2017/09/27/amazon-all-the-research-you-need-about-its-algorithm-and-innovation/.

Mattioli, Dana. "Amazon Scooped Up Data from Its Own Sellers to Launch Competing Products." *Wall Street Journal*, April 24, 2020. https://www.wsj.com/articles/amazon-scooped-up-data-from-its-own-sellers-to-launch-competing-products-11587650015.

Mattioli, Dana, and Aaron Tilley. "Amazon Has Long Ruled the Cloud. Now It Must Fend Off Rivals." *Wall Street Journal*, January 4, 2020. https://www.wsj.com/articles/amazon-has-long-ruled-the-cloud-now-it-must-fend-off-rivals-11578114008.

Milnes, Hilary. "'Trapped': How Amazon Is Cornering Fashion Brands into Wholesale." Glossy, July 10, 2017. http://www.glossy.co/the-amazon-effect/trapped-how-amazon-is-cornering-fashion-brands-into-wholesale.

Mims, Christopher. "The Limits of Amazon." *Wall Street Journal*, January 1, 2018. https://www.wsj.com/articles/the-limits-of-amazon-1514808002.

Molla, Rani, and Jason Del Rey. "Amazon's Epic 20-Year Run as a Public Company, Explained in Five Charts." Recode, May 15, 2017. https://www.recode.net/2017/5/15/15610786/amazon-jeff-bezos-public-company-profit-revenue-explained-five-charts.

Novet, Jordan. "Amazon Is in Talks to Bring Its Cashierless Go Technology to Airports and Movie Theaters." CNBC, September 30, 2019. https://www.cnbc.com/2019/09/30/amazon-go-cashierless-tech-planned-for-airport-stores-movie-theaters.html.

Palmer, Annie. "Amazon Reports Sales Growth of 37%, Topping Estimates." CNBC, October 29, 2020. https://www.cnbc.com/2020/10/29/amazon-amzn-earnings-q3-2020.html.

Pop, Valentina, and Sam Schechner. "Amazon to Face Antitrust Charges from EU over Treatment of Third-Party Sellers." *Wall Street Journal*, June 11, 2020. https://www.wsj.com/articles/amazon-to-face-antitrust-charges-from-eu-over-treatment-of-third-party-sellers-11591871818.

Reda, Susan. "21 Ways Amazon Changed the Face of Retail." *Stores Magazine*, September 2016, pp. 30–33.

Redman, Russell. "Amazon Leads in Online Grocery Shopper Satisfaction." Supermarket News, July 10, 2020. https://www.supermarketnews.com/online-retail/amazon-leads-online-grocery-shopper-satisfaction.

Rigby, Darrell K. "The Amazon–Whole Foods Deal Means Every Other Retailer's Three-Year Plan Is Obsolete." *Harvard Business Review*, June 21, 2017. https://hbr.org /2017/06/the-amazon-whole-foods-deal-means-every-other-retailers-three-year-plan -is-obsolete.

Robischon, Noah. "Why Amazon Is the World's Most Innovative Company of 2017." *Fast Company*, February 13, 2017. https://www.fastcompany.com/3067455/why -amazon-is-the-worlds-most-innovative-company-of-2017.

Ruff, Corinne. "Are Calvin Klein's Amazon Pop-Ups Dissing Department Stores?" Retail Dive, November 29, 2017. https://www.retaildive.com/news/are-calvin-kleins -amazon-pop-ups-dissing-department-stores/511700/.

Sabanoglu, Tugba. "Average Annual Amount Spent on Amazon According to U.S. Amazon Prime and Non-Prime Members as of March 2019." Statista, November 30, 2020. https://www.statista.com/statistics/304938/amazon-prime-and-non-prime -members-average-sales-spend/.

Schmid, Helen. "Competitive Strategy: Should You Compete with Amazon or Sell on Amazon?" *Harvard Business Review*, May 23, 2016. https://hbr.org/2016/05/should -you-compete-with-amazon-or-sell-on-amazon.

Schomer, Audrey. "How Amazon Advertising Is Eating Into the Digital Ad Market Currently Dominated by Google & Facebook in 2020." Business Insider, December 18, 2019. https://www.businessinsider.com/amazon-advertising-market-outlook.

Scott, Dylan. "What to Make of Amazon and Warren Buffett's Mystery Health Care Project." *Vox*, January 31, 2018. https://www.vox.com/technology/2018/1/31/16950500 /amazon-health-care-jp-morgan-chase-warren-buffett.

Siegel, Richie. "Op-Ed: Will the Digitally Native Brand Building Playbook Produce Results?" Business of Fashion, November 29, 2017. https://www.businessoffashion .com/articles/opinion/op-ed-will-the-digital-native-brand-building-playbook -produce-results.

Skrovan, Sandy. "Report: Amazon and Whole Foods to Thrive by Nabbing Each Other's Customers." Retail Dive, September 15, 2017. http://www.retaildive.com/news /report-amazon-and-whole-foods-to-thrive-by-nabbing-each-others-customers /505050/.

Soper, Spencer. "Amazon Makes It Harder for Sellers to Avoid Its Shipping Service." BNN *Bloomberg*, August 18, 2020. https://www.bnnbloomberg.ca/amazon-makes-it -harder-for-sellers-to-avoid-its-shipping-service-1.1481755.

Spector, Robert. "The Rise and Fall of Toys 'R' Us." Robin Report, October 18, 2017. http://www.therobinreport.com/the-rise-and-fall-of-toys-r-us/.

Stevens, Laura. "Amazon Delays Opening of Cashierless Store to Work Out Kinks." *Wall Street Journal*, March 27, 2017. https://www.wsj.com/articles/amazon-delays -convenience-store-opening-to-work-out-kinks-1490616133.

Stevens, Laura, and Sara Germano. "Nike Thought It Didn't Need Amazon—Then the Ground Shifted." *Wall Street Journal*, June 28, 2017. https://www.wsj.com/articles

/how-nike-resisted-amazons-dominance-for-years-and-finally-capitulated
-1498662435.

Streitfeld, David. "What Happens After Amazon's Domination Is Complete? Its Bookstore Offers Clues." *New York Times*, June 23, 2019. https://www.nytimes.com /2019/06/23/technology/amazon-domination-bookstore-books.html.

Thomas, Katie, and Claire Ballentine. "Why Amazon's Push into Prescription Drugs Isn't a Guaranteed Success." *New York Times*, July 2, 2018. https://www.nytimes.com /2018/07/02/health/amazon-pillpack-drugs.html.

Thompson, Derek. "Why Amazon Bought Whole Foods." *Atlantic*, June 16, 2017. https://www.theatlantic.com/business/archive/2017/06/why-amazon-bought-whole -foods/530652/.

Thomson, James. "Strategies to Be Successful Selling on Amazon in 2018." *International Business Times*, November 21, 2017. http://www.ibtimes.com/5 -strategies-be-successful-selling-amazon-2018-2617932.

US Securities and Exchange Commission. "2015 Letter to Shareholders." April 24, 2015. https://www.sec.gov/Archives/edgar/data/1018724/000119312516530910 /d168744dex991.htm.

Wakabayashi, Daisuke. "Prime Leverage: How Amazon Wields Power in the Technology World." *New York Times*, December 15, 2019. https://www.nytimes.com /2019/12/15/technology/amazon-aws-cloud-competition.html.

Walk-Morris, Tatiana. "Smart Speaker Shopping Falls Short of Projections." Retail Dive, February 5, 2020. https://www.retaildive.com/news/smart-speaker-shopping -falls-short-of-projections/571748/.

Weise, Karen. "Amazon Knows What You Buy. And It's Building a Big Ad Business from It." *New York Times*, January 20, 2019. https://www.nytimes.com/2019/01/20 /technology/amazon-ads-advertising.html.

———. "Amazon Wants to Rule the Grocery Aisles, and Not Just at Whole Foods." *New York Times*, July 28, 2019. https://www.nytimes.com/2019/07/28/technology /whole-foods-amazon-grocery.html.

———. "Prime Power: How Amazon Squeezes the Businesses Behind Its Store." *New York Times*, December 19, 2019. https://www.nytimes.com/2019/12/19/technology /amazon-sellers.html.

Wells, John R., Gale Danskin, and Gabriel Ellsworth. "Amazon.com, 2016." Harvard Business School Case 9-716-402. May 16, 2016. https://www.scribd.com/document /370797374/Amazon.

Whitney, Lance. "Amazon Prime Members Will Renew Despite Price Hike, Survey Finds." CNET, July 23, 2014. https://www.cnet.com/news/amazon-prime-members -will-almost-all-renew-despite-price-increase/.

Chapter 3

Bose, Nandita. "Exclusive: Aldi Raises Stakes in U.S. Price War with Wal-Mart." Reuters, May 11, 2017. http://www.reuters.com/article/us-aldi-walmart-pricing-exclusive /exclusive-aldi-raises-stakes-in-u-s-price-war-with-wal-mart-idUSKBN1870EN.

Chen, Oliver. "Target: Expect More, Pay Less . . . & Go from Crunches to Brunches." Cowen Report, August 16, 2017.

Cheng, Andria. "Dollar Stores' Growth Opportunities—and Challenges." eMarketer Retail, June 1, 2017. https://retail.emarketer.com/article/dollar-stores-growth -opportunitiesand-challenges/59308c35ebd4000b2ceae02d.

Clark, Evan, and Sharon Edelson. "Buying the Future: Amazon, Walmart Cut Deals to Compete." *WWD*, June 19, 2017. http://wwd.com/business-news/financial/amazon -wal-mart-jet-whole-foods-marc-lore-jeff-bezos-retail-ecommerce-acquisition -10917720/.

Clifford, Stephanie. "Where Wal-Mart Failed, Aldi Succeeds." *New York Times*, March 29, 2011. http://www.nytimes.com/2011/03/30/business/30aldi.html.

Corkery, Michael. "Walmart Announces Membership Service in Attempt to Compete with Amazon." *New York Times*, September 1, 2020. https://www.nytimes.com/2020 /09/01/business/walmart-plus-membership.html.

Del Rey, Jason. "Walmart Has Acquired the Logistics Startup Parcel to Help Launch Same-Day Delivery in New York City." Recode, October 3, 2017. https://www.recode .net/2017/10/3/16405158/walmart-parcel-acquisition-logistics-same-day-delivery -startup.

Economist. "Walmart: Thinking Outside the Box." June 4, 2016. https://www .economist.com/news/business/21699961-american-shoppers-move-online-walmart -fights-defend-its-dominance-thinking-outside.

Edelson, Sharon. "Wal-Mart's New Focus: Technology Is Priority, Not Super Centers." *WWD*, October 10, 2017. http://wwd.com/business-news/retail/wal-marts -2017-analyst-meeting-technology-is-buzzword-11024483/.

Hartman Group. "ALDI Is a Growing Menace to America's Grocery Retailers." *Forbes*, April 14, 2015. https://www.forbes.com/sites/thehartmangroup/2015/04/14 /aldi-is-a-growing-menace-to-americas-grocery-retailers/#42d8a711f077.

Hirsch, Lauren. "Jet Launches Its Own Private Label Brand, Uniquely J." CNBC, October 20, 2017. https://www.cnbc.com/2017/10/20/jet-launches-private-label-brand -uniquely-j.html.

Howland, Daphne. "Jet Takes on Amazon, Target with New Private Brand 'Uniquely J.'" Retail Dive, October 24, 2017. https://www.retaildive.com/news/jet-takes-on-amazon -target-with-new-private-brand-uniquely-j/507983/.

———. "Walmart Reportedly Testing Amazon Go-Like Store, Personal Shopping Service." Retail Dive, December 21, 2017. https://www.retaildive.com/news/walmart -reportedly-testing-amazon-go-like-store-personal-shopping-service/513610/.

———. "Why Walmart Is Betting Big on E-Commerce Acquisitions." Retail Dive, May 31, 2017. https://www.retaildive.com/news/why-wal-mart-is-betting-big-on-e-commerce-acquisitions/443177/.

Irwin, Neil. "The Amazon-Walmart Showdown That Explains the Modern Economy." *New York Times*, June 16, 2017. https://www.nytimes.com/2017/06/16/upshot/the-amazon-walmart-showdown-that-explains-the-modern-economy.html.

Kelleher, Kevin. "How Walmart Uses AI to Serve 140 Million Customers a Week." Venture Beat, July 11, 2017. https://venturebeat.com/2017/07/11/how-walmart-uses-ai-to-serve-140-million-customers-a-week/.

Kohan, Shelley E. "If You Can't Join Them, Buy Them!" Robin Report, September 2, 2020. https://www.therobinreport.com/if-you-cant-join-them-buy-them/?utm_source=newsletter.

Kumar, Kavita. "Target Going Ahead with Special Limited-Edition Designer Partnership on Dresses." *Star Tribune*, May 19, 2020. https://www.startribune.com/target-going-ahead-with-special-limited-edition-designer-partnership-on-dresses/570556682/.

Lewis, Robin. "Shopify Who? Ask Walmart." Robin Report, June 28, 2020. https://www.therobinreport.com/shopify-who-ask-walmart/?utm_source=newsletter.

Mattern, Jessica Leigh. "Here's the Real Reason Everyone Loves Aldi So Much." *Country Living*, October 6, 2017. http://www.countryliving.com/food-drinks/news/a45149/how-aldi-stores-work/.

Meyersohn, Nathaniel. "Walmart's Strategy to Beat Amazon." CNN, October 20, 2018. https://www.cnn.com/2018/10/19/business/walmart-stores-grocery-pickup-amazon/index.html.

Mims, Christopher. "The Next Phase of the Retail Apocalypse: Stores Reborn as E-Commerce Warehouses." *Wall Street Journal*, July 18, 2020. https://www.wsj.com/articles/the-next-phase-of-the-retail-apocalypse-stores-reborn-as-e-commerce-warehouses-11595044859.

Mondloch, Emily. "It's a New Day for Dollar Stores." Baber Martin Agency, September 15, 2017. https://www.barbermartin.com/dollar-stores-retail-expansion/ (page no longer available).

Nassauer, Sarah. "Walmart Flexes Its Scale to Power Through Pandemic." *Wall Street Journal*, August 18, 2020. https://www.wsj.com/articles/walmart-flexes-its-scale-to-power-through-pandemic-11597750961.

———. "Welcome to Walmart: The Robot Will Grab Your Groceries." *Wall Street Journal*, January 8, 2020. https://www.wsj.com/articles/welcome-to-walmart-the-robot-will-grab-your-groceries-11578499200.

———. "With His TikTok Pursuit, Walmart CEO Seeks to Revamp Retailer Again." *Wall Street Journal*, August 28, 2020. https://www.wsj.com/articles/with-his-tiktok-pursuit-walmart-ceo-seeks-to-revamp-retailer-again-11598637043.

Ochwat, Dan. "Walmart's Great Value Brand Earns More Than $27 Billion Annually." Store Brands, February 18, 2020. https://storebrands.com/walmarts-great-value-brand-earns-more-27-billion-annually.

O'Shea, Don. "How Walmart Is Using Tech This Holiday Season." Retail Dive, November 26, 2017. https://www.retaildive.com/news/how-walmart-is-using-tech-this-holiday-season/511607/.

Repko, Melissa. "Target Aims to Make Its Booming Online Business More Profitable with New Technology, Small Sort Centers." CNBC, May 20, 2020. https://www.cnbc.com/2020/05/20/heres-how-target-aims-to-make-its-booming-online-business-more-profitable.html.

Richards, Katie. "How Walmart Plans to Turn Around Its Fashion Business in 2020." Glossy, January 3, 2020. https://www.glossy.co/fashion/how-walmart-plans-to-turn-around-its-fashion-business-in-2020.

Ruff, Corinne. "Walmart's Store No. 8 Showcases the Future of VR." Retail Dive, October 19, 2017. https://www.retaildive.com/news/walmarts-store-no-8-showcases-the-future-of-vr/507639/.

Runkevicius, Dan. "Walmart Is Raising an Army of Retailers to Beat Amazon." Forbes, August 18, 2020. https://www.forbes.com/sites/danrunkevicius/2020/07/29/walmart-is-raising-an-army-of-retailers-to-beat-amazon/.

Russell, Cally. "Who Are the 10 Biggest Retailers in the World?" Forbes, January 9, 2020. https://www.forbes.com/sites/callyrussell/2020/01/09/who-are-the-10-biggest-retailers-in-the-world/.

San Juan, Rebecca. "Get Your Grocery Bags Ready: Aldi Is Adding Three South Florida Locations This Fall." Miami Herald, September 2, 2020. https://www.miamiherald.com/news/business/real-estate-news/article245410115.html.

Soper, Taylor. "How STRIVR Expanded Its VR Sport Training Platform to Walmart Associates and NFL Referees." GeekWire, August 18, 2017. https://www.geekwire.com/2017/strivr-expanded-vr-sports-training-platform-walmart-associates-nfl-referees/.

Thomas, Lauren, and Courtney Reagan. "Take That Alexa! Walmart Partners with Google to Offer Voice Shopping." CNBC, August 23, 2017. https://www.cnbc.com/2017/08/22/wal-mart-partners-with-google-to-offer-voice-shopping-via-google-home.html.

Unglesbee, Ben. "Walmart Cuts Corporate Jobs as It Focuses on Omnichannel Push." Retail Dive, July 31, 2020. https://www.retaildive.com/news/walmart-cuts-corporate-jobs-as-it-focuses-on-omnichannel-push/582691/.

———. "Walmart Sells Off 2 More Digital Brands." Retail Dive, August 28, 2020. https://www.retaildive.com/news/walmart-sells-off-2-more-digital-brands/584345/.

Weissman, Cale Guthrie. "Despite Losses, Walmart's e-Commerce Strategy Is Taking Shape." Modern Retail, January 21, 2020. https://www.modernretail.co/retailers/despite-losses-walmarts-e-commerce-strategy-is-taking-shape/.

Chapter 4

Bowman, Emma, and Sarah McCammon. "Can Fast Fashion and Sustainability Be Stitched Together?" NPR, July 27, 2019. https://www.npr.org/2019/07/27/745418569 /can-fast-fashion-and-sustainability-be-stitched-together.

Chu, Melissa. "The Unconventional Strategy Zara Used to Dominate an Industry (and What We Can Do to Mirror Its Success)." Mission, September 12, 2017. https://medium.com/the-mission/the-unconventional-strategy-zara-used-to -dominate-an-industry-and-what-we-can-do-to-mirror-its-4078698c08e0.

Dunn, Andy. "The Book of DNVB: The Rise of Digitally Native Vertical Brands." Medium, May 9, 2016. https://medium.com/@dunn/digitally-native-vertical-brands -b26a26f2cf83.

Grill-Goodman, Jamie. "Zara Parent to Close 1,200 Stores and Invest $3 Billion in E-Commerce." RIS News, June 10, 2020. https://risnews.com/zara-parent-close-1200 -stores-and-invest-3-billion-e-commerce.

Howland, Daphne. "Nordstrom Opening Merchandise-Free Concept." Retail Dive, September 11, 2017. http://www.retaildive.com/news/nordstrom-opening-merchandise -free-concept/504655/.

Interbrand. "Best Global Brands 2019." Ranking the Brands. Last accessed December 2020. https://www.rankingthebrands.com/The-Brand-Rankings.aspx ?rankingID=37&year=1273.

———. *A New Decade of Possibility: Best Global Brands 2020* (report), 2020, https:// learn.interbrand.com/hubfs/INTERBRAND/Interbrand_Best_Global_Brands%20 2020.pdf.

Jansen, Caroline. "Casper Expands Physical Presence Through Tie-up with Sam's Club." Retail Dive, August 10, 2020. https://www.retaildive.com/news/casper -expands-physical-presence-through-tie-up-with-sams-club/583220/.

Kantar. "Totaling $3.81 Trillion in Value, the BrandZ Top 100 US Brands Are Worth More Than the GDP of Germany, the Fourth Largest Economy in the World." Cision PR Newswire, November 14, 2019. https://www.prnewswire.com/news-releases /totaling-3-81-trillion-in-value-the-brandz-top-100-us-brands-are-worth-more-than -the-gdp-of-germany-the-fourth-largest-economy-in-the-world-300957486.html.

Kowsmann, Patricia. "Zara's Strategy: Bigger Stores, Online Push." MarketWatch, March 16, 2017. https://www.marketwatch.com/story/zaras-strategy-bigger-stores -online-push-2017-03-16.

Lutz, Ashley. "This Clothing Company Whose CEO Is Richer Than Warren Buffett Is Blowing the Competition Out of the Water." Business Insider, June 13, 2015. http://www.businessinsider.com/zaras-retail-strategy-is-winning-2015-6.

Mang, Lauren. "The Un-Store: High-End Stores That Don't Actually Sell Anything Are the Future of Retail." Quartz, November 24, 2017. https://qz.com/1135230/high -end-stores-that-dont-actually-sell-anything-are-the-future-of-retail/.

Neumann, Jeannette. "How Zara Is Defying a Broad Retail Slump." *Wall Street Journal*, June 14, 2017. https://www.wsj.com/articles/how-zara-is-defying-a-broad -retail-slump-1497467742.

Pixlee. *The Top 25 Digitally Native Vertical Brands 2017* (white paper), 2017, https:// www.pixlee.com/download/the-top-digitally-native-brands-report-for-2017.

PR Newswire. "Totaling $3.81 Trillion in Value, the BrandZ Top 100 US Brands Are Worth More Than the GDP of Germany, the Fourth Largest." *Bloomberg*, November 14, 2019. https://www.bloomberg.com/press-releases/2019-11-15/totaling -3-81-trillion-in-value-the-brandz-top-100-us-brands-are-worth-more-than-the-gdp -of-germany-the-fourth-largest.

Roll, Martin. "The Secret of Zara's Success: A Culture of Customer Co-Creation." Martin Roll Business & Brand Leadership, December 2016. https://martinroll.com /resources/articles/strategy/the-secret-of-zaras-success-a-culture-of-customer-co -creation/.

Self, Angela. "Getting the Inside Scoop on Mattress Pricing." *Globe and Mail*, June 2, 2011. https://www.theglobeandmail.com/globe-investor/personal-finance/getting-the -inside-scoop-on-mattress-pricing/article581813/.

Siegel, Richie. "From a Digitally-Native Gold Rush to an Impending Bloodbath." Loose Threads, October 20, 2017. https://loosethreads.com/espresso/2017/10/19 /digitally-native-gold-rush-impending-bloodbath/.

———. "Op-Ed: Will the Digitally Native Brand Building Playbook Produce Results?" Business of Fashion, November 29, 2017. https://www.businessoffashion.com/articles /opinion/op-ed-will-the-digital-native-brand-building-playbook-produce-results.

Slane, Kevin. "Trader Joe's Won't Offer Online Ordering, Grocery Delivery, or Curbside Pickup: Here's Why." *Boston Globe*, April 24, 2020. https://www.boston.com /food/coronavirus/2020/04/24/trader-joes-online-ordering-delivery.

Taylor, Kate. "Whole Foods Is Cutting Prices—and It's Hitting Trader Joe's Hard." Business Insider, October 3, 2017. http://www.businessinsider.com/amazon-buys -whole-foods-hurts-trader-joes-target-2017-10.

Trader Joe's. "Our Story" (homepage). Accessed February 25, 2018. https://www .traderjoes.com/our-story.

Varma, Ankita. "Zara's Secret to Success Lies in Big Data and an Agile Supply Chain." *Straits Times*, May 25, 2017. http://www.straitstimes.com/lifestyle/fashion/zaras -secret-to-success-lies-in-big-data-and-an-agile-supply-chain.

Welch, Liz. "How Casper Became a $100 Million Company in Less Than Two Years." *Inc.*, February 25, 2016. https://www.inc.com/magazine/201603/liz-welch/casper -changing-mattress-industry.html.

Wilson, Marianne. "Hot Online Mattress Start-Up Delves into Brick-and-Mortar." Chain Store Age, November 1, 2017. https://www.chainstoreage.com/store-spaces/hot -online-mattress-start-delves-brick-mortar/.

Wohletz, Jenn. "Top Five Reasons Why People Love Trader Joe's So F*@%ing Much." Westword, February 17, 2012. http://www.westword.com/restaurants/top-five-reasons-why-people-love-trader-joes-so-f-ing-much-5773473.

Chapter 5

Alvarez, Edgar. "The World of High Fashion Finally Has Its Answer to Amazon." Engadget, July 13, 2017. https://www.engadget.com/2017/07/13/lvmh-24-sevres-interview/.

Bain & Company. "Global Personal Luxury Goods Market Returns to Health Growth, Reaching a Fresh High of 262 Billion Euros in 2017." October 25, 2017. http://www.bain.com/about/press/press-releases/press-release-2017-global-fall-luxury-market-study.aspx.

Berezhna, Victoria. "The Art of the Markdown." Business of Fashion, December 15, 2017. https://www.businessoffashion.com/articles/intelligence/the-art-of-the-markdown.

Berthon, Pierre, Leyland F. Pitt, Michael Parent, and Jean-Paul Berthon. "Aesthetics and Ephemerality: Observing and Preserving the Luxury Brand." *California Management Review* 52, no. 1 (November 2009): 45–66. https://doi.org/10.1525/cmr.2009.52.1.45.

Binkley, Christina. "At Luxury Stores, It Isn't Shopping, It's an Experience." *Wall Street Journal*, April 16, 2017. https://www.wsj.com/articles/at-luxury-stores-it-isnt-shopping-its-an-experience-1492394460.

BOF Team. "The BoF Podcast: Neiman Marcus Chief Executive Sees Stores as Vital for Digital Growth." Business of Fashion, July 16, 2020. https://www.businessoffashion.com/articles/podcasts/the-bof-podcast-neiman-marcus-chief-executive-sees-stores-as-vital-for-digital-growth.

———. "Karl Lagerfeld's Greatest Legacy Is a Business Model." Business of Fashion, February 22, 2019. https://www.businessoffashion.com/articles/professional/karl-lagerfelds-greatest-legacy-is-a-business-model-chanel.

———. "What Fashion Needs to Know from Mary Meeker's 2019 Internet Trends Report." Business of Fashion, June 14, 2019. https://www.businessoffashion.com/articles/professional/what-fashion-needs-to-know-from-mary-meekers-2019-internet-trends-report?utm_source=daily-digest-newsletter.

Clark, Evan. "Louis Vuitton x Supreme: A 100M Euro Boost for Skate Brand's Luxe Cred." *WWD*, October 13, 2017. http://wwd.com/business-news/financial/louis-vuitton-supreme-carlyle-100m-skate-brand-luxury-11026636/.

Danziger, Pamela N. "Luxury Brands Innovation Is No Luxury, but a Necessity." *Forbes*, August 8, 2017. https://www.forbes.com/sites/pamdanziger/2017/08/08/luxury-brands-innovation-is-no-luxury-but-a-necessity/2/#4876cf9c4be5.

———. "3 Ways Millennials and Gen-Z Consumers Are Radically Transforming the Luxury Market." *Forbes*, May 29, 2019. https://www.forbes.com/sites/pamdanziger

/2019/05/29/3-ways-millennials-and-gen-z-consumers-are-radically-transforming
-the-luxury-market/.

Doupnik, Elizabeth. "2018 Retail Predictions: AI, Experiences, Pricing Transparency
to Increase." *WWD*, December 4, 2017. http://wwd.com/business-news/retail/edited
-2018-retail-forecast-11062611/.

Esposito, Alicia. "How Luxury Brands Are Responding to COVID Tension with
Innovation." Retail Reset, July 9, 2020. https://retailtouchpoints.com/topics/how
-luxury-brands-are-responding-to-covid-tension-with-innovation.

Fernandez, Chantal. "Farfetch Sales Soared During Lockdowns." Business of
Fashion, August 14, 2020. https://www.businessoffashion.com/articles/professional
/farfetch-results-q2-2020-coronavirus-luxury-fashion-ecommerce.

———. "The Problem with the Online Luxury Model." Business of Fashion, May 14,
2020. https://www.businessoffashion.com/articles/professional/the-problem-with-the
-online-luxury-model.

———. "What Luxury Can Do About the Tourism Crisis." Business of Fashion,
July 20, 2020. https://www.businessoffashion.com/articles/professional/travel-luxury
-coronavirus-ecommerce-china-luxury-tourism-duty-free.

Fontana, Roberto, Stéphan J. G. Girod, and Martin Králik. "How Luxury Brands Can
Beat Counterfeiters." *Harvard Business Review*, May 24, 2019. https://hbr.org/2019/05
/how-luxury-brands-can-beat-counterfeiters.

Grigorian, Greg. "Luxury Brands Are Digitizing, and China Is Their Fiercest Digitizer."
Pandaily, December 17, 2019. https://pandaily.com/luxury-brands-are-digitizing
-and-china-is-their-fiercest-digitizer/.

Halzack, Sarah. "American Luxury Brands Remember to Be Luxurious." Bloomberg
Gadfly, November 6, 2017. https://www.bloomberg.com/gadfly/articles/2017-11-06
/michael-kors-earnings-luxury-wins-by-being-luxurious.

Han, Young Jee, Joseph C. Nunes, and Xavier Drèze. "Signaling Status with Luxury
Goods: The Role of Brand Prominence." *Journal of Marketing* 74, no. 4 (July 2010):
15–30. https://doi.org/10.1509/jmkg.74.4.015.

Howland, Daphne. "Coach Rebrands as 'Tapestry.'" Retail Dive, October 12, 2017.
http://www.retaildive.com/news/coach-rebrands-as-tapestry/507146/.

———. "The Comeback of the Brick-and-Mortar Store." Retail Dive, January 13, 2020.
https://www.retaildive.com/news/the-comeback-of-the-brick-and-mortar-store
/570290/.

———. "Nordstrom Says 'Local' Stores Are Its Future." Retail Dive, May 22, 2019.
https://www.retaildive.com/news/nordstrom-says-local-stores-are-its-future/555321/.

Kansara, Vikram Alexei. "Amid Pandemic, Luxury Leaders Seize Digital
Opportunity to Gain on Rivals." Business of Fashion, July 31, 2020. https://www
.businessoffashion.com/articles/professional/luxury-coronavirus-digital-lvmh
-kering-prada-q2-2020-results.

Kapferer, J. N. *Kapferer on Luxury: How Luxury Brands Can Grow yet Remain Rare.* Philadelphia: Kogan Page, 2015.

Knowledge@Wharton. "How Digital Retailers Opening Physical Stores Increases Sales." 2019. https://knowledge.wharton.upenn.edu/article/digital-retailers-opening -physical-stores/.

La Ferla, Ruth. "The Cult of the Line: It's Not About the Merch." *New York Times,* August 3, 2017. https://www.nytimes.com/2017/08/03/fashion/waiting-in-line -supreme-streetwear-merch.html.

Menkes, Suzy. "Retail Is Broken: Angela Ahrendts Has a Plan." *Vogue Business,* January 28, 2019. https://www.voguebusiness.com/companies/angela-ahrendts-apple -retail-strategy.

Milnes, Hilary. "How China's Luxury E-Commerce Market Will Evolve in 2018." Glossy, December 15, 2017. http://www.glossy.co/year-in-review/how-chinas-luxury -e-commerce-market-will-evolve-in-2018.

O'Connor, Tamison. "Selling Fashion to the 1% During a Pandemic." Business of Fashion, August 4, 2020. https://www.businessoffashion.com/articles/professional /selling-fashion-to-the-1-during-a-pandemic.

Paton, Elizabeth. "Europe's Luxury Retailers May Be Returning to Form." *New York Times,* July 28, 2017. https://www.nytimes.com/2017/07/28/business/luxury-brands -europe-gucci-lvmh.html.

———. "Imagining the Retail Store of the Future." *New York Times,* April 12, 2017. https://www.nytimes.com/2017/04/12/fashion/store-of-the-future.html.

———. "LVMH and the Next Big Digital Shopping Experience." *New York Times,* May 10, 2017. https://www.nytimes.com/2017/05/10/fashion/lvmh-ian-rogers-24 -sevres-takes-on-amazon.html.

Puleo, Melissa. "The Secret Rise of Digital Strategy for Luxury Brands." Decoded: Contemporary Commerce, October 24, 2017. https://www.salsify.com/blog/digital -strategy-for-luxury-brands.

Salpini, Cara. "Study: Gen Z More Likely Than Millennials to Buy Luxury Brands." Retail Dive, July 7, 2017. https://www.retaildive.com/news/study-gen-z-more-likely -than-millennials-to-buy-luxury-brands/446623/.

Sherman, Lauren. "Chanel Sees Trouble Through 2021: What Happens Now?" Business of Fashion, June 18, 2020. https://www.businessoffashion.com/articles /professional/chanel-surpasses-12-billion-in-2019-sales.

———. "Marc Jacobs to Close London Store and Other European Outposts." Business of Fashion, January 5, 2018. https://www.businessoffashion.com/articles/news -analysis/marc-jacobs-to-close-london-store-and-other-european-outposts.

———. "The Next Wave of Luxury E-Commerce." Business of Fashion, April 2020. https://courses.businessoffashion.com/courses/take/case-study-luxury-ecommerce -online-retail/pdfs/11481339-the-next-wave-of-luxury-e-commerce.

———. "Winners Take All: How LVMH and Kering Will Extend Their Supremacy Post-pandemic." Business of Fashion, May 26, 2020. https://www.businessoffashion .com/articles/professional/winners-take-all-how-lvmh-and-kering-will-extend-their -supremacy-post-pandemic?utm_source=daily-digest-newsletter.

———. "Yoox Net-a-Porter's 'Painful' Tech Upgrade Drags Down Richemont." Business of Fashion, November 18, 2019. https://www.businessoffashion.com/articles /professional/yoox-net-a-porter-richemont-tech.

Smith, Katie. "The Retail Landscape in 2018." Edited, December 21, 2017. https:// edited.com/blog/2017/12/retail-trends-of-2018/.

Solca, Luca. "How Luxury Brands Sell 'Exclusive' Goods by the Millions." Business of Fashion, June 22, 2020. https://www.businessoffashion.com/articles/professional /luxury-exclusivity-pricing-chanel-louis-vuitton-dior.

Suen, Zoe. "How the Wholesale Crisis Could Benefit Independent Fashion Brands." Business of Fashion, July 10, 2020. https://www.businessoffashion.com/articles /professional/wholesale-crisis-could-benefit-independent-fashion-brands-galeries -lafayette-burberry-selfridges.

Thomas, Lauren. "Michael Kors Hikes 2018 Outlook, Sending Shares of the Handbag Maker Higher." CNBC, November 6, 2017. https://www.cnbc.com/2017/11/06 /michael-kors-hikes-2018-outlook-sending-luxury-retailers-shares-up.html.

Wahba, Phil. "Coach Thinks Outside the Bag." Fortune, May 24, 2017. http://fortune .com/2017/05/24/coach-victor-luis-stuart-vevers/.

Chapter 6

Baird-Remba, Rebecca. "Are Off-Price Retailers Truly Amazon-Proof?" Commercial Observer, December 7, 2017. https://commercialobserver.com/2017/12/are-off-price -retailers-truly-amazon-proof/.

Bhattarai, Abha. "Will Millennials Kill Costco?" Washington Post, January 19, 2018. https://www.washingtonpost.com/business/economy/will-millennials-kill-costco /2018/01/19/d0de5dec-fb9e-11e7-a46b-a3614530bd87_story.html.

Bloomberg. "The TJ Maxx Strategy: How One Huge American Retailer Ignored the Internet and Won." Business of Fashion, December 21, 2016. https://www .businessoffashion.com/articles/news-analysis/how-one-huge-american-retailer -ignored-the-internet-and-won.

Cuozzo, Steve. "The Complex Economics of NYC's Food Hall Glut." New York Post, January 18, 2018. https://nypost.com/2018/01/18/the-complex-economics-of-nycs -food-hall-glut/.

Estes, Diane Lincoln. "In the Age of Amazon, an Entrepreneur Explains What Will Make Us Want to Go to the Store." PBS NewsHour, August 24, 2017. https://www.pbs.org /newshour/economy/age-amazon-entrepreneur-explains-will-make-us-want-go-store.

Filloon, Whitney. "Eataly Eyes IPO in 2018." Eater, December 11, 2017. https://www .eater.com/2017/12/11/16762716/eataly-ipo-2018.

———. "How Eataly Became an Italian Food Superpower." Eater, October 30, 2017. https://www.eater.com/2016/8/12/12442512/eataly-history-store-locations.

Gerstell, Emily, Sophie Marchessou, Jennifer Schmidt, and Emma Spagnuolo. "How COVID-19 Is Changing the World of Beauty." McKinsey & Company, May 8, 2020. https://www.mckinsey.com/industries/consumer-packaged-goods/our-insights/how -COVID-19-is-changing-the-world-of-beauty.

Gibson, Ellen. "Hidden Treasures Drive Impulse Buys: Surprises in Stores Lure Customers to Spend More." Boston.com, July 6, 2011. http://archive.boston.com /business/articles/2011/07/06/hidden_treasures_drive_impulse_buys/.

Gonzalez, Angel, and Janet I. Tu. "Is Amazon a Threat to Costco? Survey Weighs Coexistence." Seattle Times, October 26, 2016. https://www.seattletimes.com /business/amazon/rivals-amazon-costco-can-both-thrive-survey-says/.

Howland, Daphne. "Costco 'Destroys' November with Massive Sales Surge." Retail Dive, November 30, 2017. https://www.retaildive.com/news/costco-destroys-november -with-massive-sales-surge/511990/.

———. "Costco Sales Soar 14.3% in December." Retail Dive, January 5, 2018. https://www.retaildive.com/news/costco-sales-soar-143-in-december/514141/.

Kestenbaum, Richard. "Soaring Off-Price Retail Chains May Be Set for a Fall." Forbes, November 15, 2017. https://www.forbes.com/sites/richardkestenbaum/2017/11 /15/the-off-price-business-is-more-troubled-than-it-looks/#26ffa9ed1554.

Kowitt, Beth. "Is T.J. Maxx the Best Retail Store in the Land?" Fortune, July 24, 2014. http://fortune.com/2014/07/24/t-j-maxx-the-best-retail-store/.

Liu, Evie. "There's One 'Unquestioned' Leader in Grocery Prices." Barron's, October 13, 2017. https://www.barrons.com/articles/theres-one-unquestioned-leader-in-grocery -prices-1507927977.

Loeb, Walter. "Costco Looks for the New Normal After First COVID-19 Wave." Forbes, May 29, 2020. https://www.forbes.com/sites/walterloeb/2020/05/29/costco -looks-for-the-new-normal-after-first-covid-19-wave/?sh=192b822c2adb.

Mahoney, Sarah. "Buoyed by Instacart, Costco Seems Amazon-Proof." Marketing Daily, December 18, 2017. https://www.mediapost.com/publications/article/311803 /buoyed-by-instacart-costco-seems-amazon-proof.html.

Meyrowitz, Carol. "How I Did It: The CEO of TJX on How to Train." Harvard Business Review, May 2014. Reprint R1405A.

Milnes, Hilary. "How Tech in Rebecca Minkoff's Fitting Rooms Tripled Expected Clothing Sales." Digiday, September 25, 2015. https://digiday.com/marketing/rebecca -minkoff-digital-store/.

———. "Rebecca Minkoff Uses VR for Planning Stores." Glossy, November 30, 2017. http://www.glossy.co/store-of-the-future/rebecca-minkoff-uses-vr-for-planning-stores.

Nassauer, Sarah. "How Kirkland Signature Became One of Costco's Biggest Success Stories." Wall Street Journal, September 10, 2017. https://www.wsj.com/articles/how -kirkland-signature-became-one-of-costcos-biggest-success-stories-1505041202.

O'Connor, Clare. "No Trick, Just Treat: Halloween Pop-Ups Now Account for Half Spencer Gifts' Annual Sales." *Forbes*, October 11, 2013. https://www.forbes.com/sites/clareoconnor/2013/10/11/no-trick-just-treat-halloween-pop-ups-now-account-for-half-spencer-gifts-annual-sales/#48baf6ff317a.

Pasquarelli, Adrianne. "How TJX Crafted a Winning Marketing Playbook." *Ad Age*, May 23, 2016. http://adage.com/article/cmo-strategy/award-find-retailer-winning/304117/.

Salpini, Cara. "30 Minutes with Sephora's Head of Marketing." Retail Dive, November 29, 2017. https://www.retaildive.com/news/30-minutes-with-sephoras-head-of-marketing/510300/.

———. "Will Amazon Give Beauty a Makeover?" Retail Dive, January 11, 2018. https://www.retaildive.com/news/will-amazon-give-beauty-a-makeover/514544/.

Thomas, Lauren. "Pop-Up Shop Pioneer Spirit Halloween Is Hitting the Mall as More Retailers Vacate." CNBC, October 5, 2017. https://www.cnbc.com/2017/10/05/halloween-pop-up-shops-expand-us-footprint-other-retailers-vacate.html.

Twilley, Nicola, and Cynthia Graber. "A Glimpse into the World's First Italian-Food Theme Park." *Atlantic*, October 23, 2017. https://www.theatlantic.com/science/archive/2017/10/eataly-future-of-supermarkets/543678/.

Valuewalk. "Costco Wholesale: A Standout in the Saturated Retail Sector." Yahoo! Finance, March 30, 2020. https://finance.yahoo.com/news/costco-wholesale-standout-saturated-retail-190957105.html.

Walker, Rob. "Why TJ Maxx Doesn't Need E-Commerce to Survive the Pandemic." Marker, August 6, 2020. https://marker.medium.com/why-tj-maxx-doesnt-need-e-commerce-to-survive-the-pandemic-2b9cb766cedc?gi=sd.

Wells, Jeff. "Costco's Strong Q1 Earnings Prove It's Still Amazon-Proof." Retail Dive, December 15, 2017. https://www.retaildive.com/news/costcos-strong-q1-earnings-prove-its-still-amazon-proof/513185/.

Wolf, Liz. "Beauty Retailers Face New Challenges Post-COVID." National Real Estate Investor, June 17, 2020. https://www.nreionline.com/retail/beauty-retailers-face-new-challenges-post-covid.

Yohn, Denise Lee. "Big-Box Retailers Have Two Options If They Want to Survive." *Harvard Business Review*, June 22, 2016. https://hbr.org/2016/06/big-box-retailers-have-two-options-if-they-want-to-survive.

Chapter 7

Alibaba. "Rules List." Accessed 2020. https://rule.alibaba.com/rule/rule_list/146.htm.

Alibaba Group. "History and Milestones." Accessed 2020. https://www.alibabagroup.com/en/about/history?year=2004.

Alizila Staff. "What China Reveals About the Future of Shopping." Alizila, May 4, 2017. https://www.alizila.com/china-reveals-future-shopping/.

Bain, Marc. "The Unique Challenges of Selling Fashion in China." Quartz, January 15, 2020. https://qz.com/1785406/allbirds-and-tmall-on-the-challenges-of -selling-fashion-in-china/.

Beall, Abigail. "In China, the Prestige of Online Shopping Is Fuelling a Debt Crisis." *WIRED UK*, February 1, 2019. https://www.wired.co.uk/article/china-debt-crisis -mianzi.

Benji. "The Secret to Successful E-Commerce in China." Marketing To China, June 22, 2017. https://www.marketingtochina.com/secret-successful-e-commerce -china/.

Biggs, Chris, Amee Chande, Erica Matthews, Pierre Mercier, Angela Wang, and Linda Zou. "What China Reveals About the Future of Shopping." BCG, May 4, 2017. https://www.bcg.com/en-us/publications/2017/retail-globalization-china-reveals -future-shopping.

Bloomberg News. "Tencent-Backed Little Red Book Seeks $6 Billion Valuation." *Bloomberg*, January 10, 2020. https://www.bloomberg.com/news/articles/2020-01-10 /tencent-backed-little-red-book-said-to-seek-6-billion-valuation.

Blystone, Dan. "Understanding the Alibaba Business Model." Investopedia, August 28, 2020. https://www.investopedia.com/articles/investing/062315/understanding -alibabas-business-model.asp.

Bradshaw, Tim, and Hannah Murphy. "TikTok Explores Curated Content Feed to Lure Advertisers." *Financial Times*, January 13, 2020. https://www.ft.com/content /e1e6baf6-34ba-11ea-a6d3-9a26f8c3cba4.

Bryant, Sue. "10 Cultural Differences Between the Chinese and Americans." Country Navigator, July 17, 2019. https://countrynavigator.com/blog/global-talent/cultural -differences-us-vs-china/.

Chou, Christine. "Cartier Launches New Store on Tmall Luxury Pavilion." Alizila, January 10, 2020. https://www.alizila.com/cartier-launches-new-store-on-tmall -luxury-pavilion/.

Cirisano, Tatiana. "TikTok Is Rewriting How Hits Get Made." *Billboard*, January 10, 2020. https://www.billboard.com/articles/business/8547681/tik-tok-app-biggest -music-hits-2020-analysis.

D'Onfro, Jillian. "How Jack Ma Went from Being a Poor School Teacher to Turning Alibaba into a $160 Billion Behemoth." Business Insider, September 14, 2014. https://www.businessinsider.com/the-story-of-jack-ma-founder-of-alibaba-2014-9.

eMarketer. "eMarketer Projects Surge in Mobile Payments in China." November 2, 2017. https://www.emarketer.com/Article/eMarketer-Projects-Surge-Mobile -Payments-China/1016695.

Engen, John. "Why China's Mobile Payments Revolution Matters for U.S. Bankers." American Banker, April 29, 2018. https://www.americanbanker.com/news/why -chinas-mobile-payments-revolution-matters-for-us-bankers.

Grothaus, Michael. "Alibaba Says Singles Day Sales Brought in a Record $31 Billion This Year." *Fast Company*, November 11, 2019. https://www.fastcompany.com /90428906/alibaba-says-singles-day-sales-brought-in-a-record-31-billion-this-year.

Gupta, Ruchi. "Just How Far Ahead Is Alibaba in China's e-Commerce Market?" Market Realist, July 17, 2019. https://marketrealist.com/2019/07/just-how-far-ahead -is-alibaba-in-chinas-e-commerce-market/.

Hallanan, Lauren. "5 Chinese Marketing Terms You Must Know in 2020." *Forbes*, January 7, 2020. https://www.forbes.com/sites/laurenhallanan/2020/01/07/5-chinese -marketing-terms-you-must-know-in-2020/?sh=257970c939c6.

JD.com. "JD.com Speeds Package Deliveries with New Parcel Delivery Service for Chinese Consumers." PR Newswire, October 25, 2018. https://www.prnewswire.com /news-releases/jdcom-speeds-package-deliveries-with-new-parcel-delivery-service -for-chinese-consumers-300738254.html.

Keyes, Daniel, and Greg Magana. "Chinese Fintechs Like Ant Financial's Alipay and Tencent's WeChat Are Rapidly Growing Their Financial Services Ecosystems." Business Insider, December 18, 2019, https://www.businessinsider.com/china-fintech -alipay-wechat.

Kharpal, Arjun. "Alibaba and JD.com Handle a Record $136.51 Billion in Sales During Major Chinese Shopping Event." CNBC, June 19, 2020. https://www.cnbc .com/2020/06/19/alibaba-jdcom-handle-record-sales-during-618-event.html.

———. "Everything You Need to Know About WeChat—China's Billion-User Messaging App." CNBC, February 3, 2019. https://www.cnbc.com/2019/02/04/what -is-wechat-china-biggest-messaging-app.html.

Klebnikov, Sergei. "Alibaba's 11/11 Singles' Day by the Numbers: A Record $38 Billion Haul." *Forbes*, November 11, 2019. https://www.forbes.com/sites/sergeiklebnikov /2019/11/11/alibabas-1111-singles-day-by-the-numbers-a-record-38-billion-haul/?sh =4a5f43012772.

Liang, Lim Yan. "Fake Goods Weeded Out Successfully on Taobao: Alibaba." *Straits Times*, January 16, 2019. https://www.straitstimes.com/asia/fake-goods-weeded-out -successfully-on-taobao-alibaba.

Lee, Emma. "Content Emerges as New Driver of Chinese e-Commerce." TechNode, May 14, 2019. https://technode.com/2019/05/14/content-emerges-as-new-driver-of -chinese-e-commerce/.

Levy, Adam. "Amazon Could Still Gain E-Commerce Market Share in 2020." Motley Fool, June 10, 2020. https://www.fool.com/investing/2020/06/10/amazon-still-gain-e -commerce-market-share-in-2020.aspx.

Liao, Rita. "Alibaba and Amazon Move Over, We Visited JD's Connected Grocery Store in China." TechCrunch, November 16, 2018. https://techcrunch.com/2018/11/15 /jd-7fresh-supermarket/.

———. "Pinduoduo Cements Position as China's Second-Largest Ecommerce Player." TechCrunch, June 27, 2019. https://techcrunch.com/2019/06/26/pinduoduo-second -biggest-china-ecommerce/.

Lim, Shawn. "Emerging Platforms: What Is Xiaohongshu and How Can Brands Leverage It?" Drum, March 16, 2020. https://www.thedrum.com/news/2020/03/16 /emerging-platforms-what-xiaohongshu-and-how-can-brands-leverage-it.

Luan, Lan, Aimee Kim, Daniel Zipser, Minyi Su, Adrian Lo, Cherry Chen, and Cherie Zhang. *China Luxury Report 2019*, 2019, https://www.mckinsey.com/~/media /mckinsey/featured%20insights/china/how%20young%20chinese%20consumers%20 are%20reshaping%20global%20luxury/mckinsey-china-luxury-report-2019-how -young-chinese-consumers-are-reshaping-global-luxury.ashx.

Luo Chao Channel. "Taobao Launches Short Video App Luke: There Is No Heart-Shaking Heart, but There Is a Heart-Shaking Heart." 36Kr, September 19, 2018. https://36kr.com/p/1722843742209.

Ma, Jack. "'Unparalleled Ruthlessness' Awaits: Jack Ma's Letter to Alibaba Employees." *Wall Street Journal*, May 7, 2014. https://www.wsj.com/articles/BL-CJB -21993.

Ma, Yihan. "Leading B2C Retailers' Share of Sales in Total Retail e-Commerce Sales in China in 2019." Statista, July 22, 2020. https://www.statista.com/statistics/880212 /sales-share-of-the-leading-e-commerce-retailers-in-china/.

Mars Culture, Institute of New Rank, Caas Data, and CBN Data. "2019 短视频内容营销趋势白皮书." CBNData, April 8, 2019. https://www.cbndata.com/report/1430/detail ?isReading=report.

Meena, Satish, and Ziaofeng Wang. "China Shopper Insights and the Impact of Covid-19." Forrester, May 29, 2020. https://www.forrester.com/report/China+Shoppe r+Insights+And+The+Impact+Of+COVID19/-/E-RES160758.

Mingyue Zeng. "Empirical Analysis of Chinese Consumers' Attitudes and Value Perceptions on Luxury Brands." Business administration. Université Côte d'Azur, 2018. English. ffNNT : 2018AZUR0034ff. fftel-02022823f.

Najberg, Adam. "Tmall Leads the Charge for Quality Consumption in China." Alizila, June 14, 2017. https://www.alizila.com/tmall-leads-the-charge-for-quality -consumption-in-china.

Nie, Winter, and Yunfei Feng. "Pinduoduo, China's Social e-Commerce Company, Is at a Crossroads." IMD Business School, February 4, 2019. https://www.imd.org /research-knowledge/articles/pdd-ecommerce-for-the-underserved/.

Ninia, John. "The United States Lags Behind China in Adopting Mobile Payments: BusinessFeed." Cornell SC Johnson, October 23, 2019. https://business.cornell.edu /hub/2019/10/23/united-states-china-mobile-payments/.

Pham, Sherisse. "Chinese Shoppers Are Staying Online: That's Great News for JD .com." CNN, June 19, 2020. https://www.cnn.com/2020/06/18/tech/jd-618-china -coronavirus-intl-hnk/index.html.

Phil K. "Alibaba's New Retail Net Profit Exceeded Expectations by 262.1% in Q2." Produce Report, December 1, 2019. https://www.producereport.com/article/alibabas -new-retail-net-profit-exceeded-expectations-2621-q2.

Scully, Jules. "Unilever Partners with JD.com to Expand Its Reach in China." FoodBev Media, August 16, 2018. https://www.foodbev.com/news/unilever-partners -with-jd-com-to-expand-its-reach-in-china/.

Singh, Manish. "Alibaba to Invest $3.3B to Bump Its Stake in Logistics Unit Cainiao." TechCrunch, November 8, 2019. https://techcrunch.com/2019/11/08/alibaba-cainiao -63-percent/.

Soo, Zen. "Why Open a Store? Chinese Merchants Go Livestreaming Instead." ABC News, May 14, 2020. https://abcnews.go.com/Technology/wireStory/open-store -chinese-merchants-livestreaming-70673422.

Stein, Pete. "What US Marketers Can Learn from Social Commerce in China." *Forbes*, August 7, 2014. https://www.forbes.com/sites/onmarketing/2014/08/07/what -us-marketers-can-learn-from-social-commerce-in-china/.

Theodosi, Natalie. "Changes Afoot at Farfetch: New Management, China Push, Start-up Investments." *WWD*, June 11, 2019. https://wwd.com/business-news/retail /changes-afoot-at-farfetch-new-management-china-push-start-up-investments -1203165605/.

Van Rompaey, Stefan. "Say Hello to 7Fresh, JD.com's High-Tech Supermarket." RetailDetail, April 1, 2020. https://www.retaildetail.eu/en/news/food/say-hello-7fresh -jdcoms-high-tech-supermarket.

Wang, Yue. "JD.com Goes All Out for Market Share, but Margins May Shrink." *Forbes*, May 21, 2020. https://www.forbes.com/sites/ywang/2020/05/21/jdcom-goes -all-out-for-market-share-but-margins-may-shrink/.

Weinswig, Deborah. "What Chinese Consumers Want from Western Retailers (Hint: It's Not Just Fashion and Technology)." *Forbes*, May 18, 2018. https://www.forbes.com /sites/deborahweinswig/2018/05/18/chinas-116b-cross-border-market-shows -sustained-potential-for-grocery-beauty-healthcare-brands/.

Wei Wei. "BAT+ 头条占据七成移动互联网使用时长_用户." Sohu, April 24, 2019. https://www.sohu.com/a/310012220_115865.

Yi, Ding. "Money-Losing Pinduoduo Overtakes JD.com as China's Second Most Valuable Online Retailer." CX Tech. Caixin Global, May 13, 2020. https://www .caixinglobal.com/2020-05-13/money-losing-pinduoduo-overtakes-jdcom-as-chinas -second-most-valuable-online-retailer-101553661.html.

Zhang, Jane. "Social Commerce Taking Larger Share of China's Online Retail Sales." *South China Morning Post*, June 12, 2020. https://www.scmp.com/tech/e-commerce /article/3088788/social-commerce-taking-larger-share-chinas-online-retail-sales.

Zheng, Ker. "Eight Things That Rocked China E-Commerce in 2019." Jing Daily, December 25, 2019. https://jingdaily.com/eight-things-that-rocked-china-e -commerce-in-2019/.

Zheng, Ruonan. "Livestream Goldmine: Kim Kardashian Meets Chinese Top Livestreamer Viya." Jing Daily, November 10, 2019, https://jingdaily.com/livesteam -goldmine-kim-kardashian-meets-chinese-top-livestreamer-viya/.

Conclusion

Fernandez, Chantal. "J.Crew, Gap, Abercrombie & Fitch: The Trouble with America's Most Beloved Mall Brands." Business of Fashion, January 9, 2017. https://www .businessoffashion.com/articles/intelligence/gap-j-crew-abercrombie-trouble -americas-mall-brands.

Ruff, Corinne. "7 Retail Execs Envision the Future of Stores." Retail Dive, February 13, 2018. https://www.retaildive.com/news/7-retail-execs-envision-the -future-of-stores/516795/.

Wahba, Phil. "Gap Inc. Is Closing 200 Stores but Opening 270 New Ones." *Fortune*, September 6, 2017. http://fortune.com/2017/09/06/gap-inc-banana-republic-old-navy/.

———. "Macy's Sales Decline for the 10th Straight Quarter." *Fortune*, August 10, 2017. http://fortune.com/2017/08/10/macys-sales-decline-2/.

Index

Page numbers in italics indicate figures.

About the Author

Barbara E. Kahn is Patty and Jay H. Baker Professor of Marketing at the Wharton School at the University of Pennsylvania. She served two terms as the director of the Jay H. Baker Retailing Center. She served as executive director of the Marketing Science Institute (MSI) (2019–2021). Before rejoining Wharton in 2011, Barbara served as the dean and Schein Professor of Marketing at the School of Business Administration, University of Miami (from 2007 to 2011). Before becoming dean at UM, she spent 17 years at Wharton as Silberberg Professor of Marketing. She was also vice dean of the Wharton undergraduate program.

Barbara is an internationally recognized scholar on retailing, variety seeking, brand loyalty, product assortment and design, and consumer and patient decision-making. She has published more than 75 articles in leading academic journals. In addition to *The Shopping Revolution*, she is the author of *Global Brand Power: Leveraging Branding for Long-Term Growth* and coauthor of *Grocery Revolution: The New Focus on the Consumer.*

Barbara has been elected president of the Association for Consumer Research, elected president of the Journal of Consumer Research (JCR) Policy Board, and selected as an MSI trustee. She was also an associate editor at *JCR*, *Journal of Marketing*, and *Marketing Science*. She was elected as a fellow for both the Association of Consumer Research and the Society of Consumer Psychology.

Barbara received her PhD, MBA, and MPhil from Columbia University, and her BA from the University of Rochester.

About Wharton School Press

Wharton School Press, the book publishing arm of the Wharton School of the University of Pennsylvania, was established to inspire bold, insightful thinking within the global business community.

Wharton School Press publishes a select list of award-winning, best-selling, and thought-leading books that offer trusted business knowledge to help leaders at all levels meet the challenges of today and the opportunities of tomorrow. Led by a spirit of innovation and experimentation, Wharton School Press leverages groundbreaking digital technologies and has pioneered a fast-reading business book format that fits readers' busy lives, allowing them to swiftly emerge with the tools and information needed to make an impact. Wharton School Press books offer guidance and inspiration on a variety of topics, including leadership, management, strategy, innovation, entrepreneurship, finance, marketing, social impact, public policy, and more.

Wharton School Press also operates an online bookstore featuring a curated selection of influential books by Wharton School faculty and Press authors published by a wide range of leading publishers.

To find books that will inspire and empower you to increase your impact and expand your personal and professional horizons, visit *wsp.wharton.upenn.edu.*

About the Wharton School

Founded in 1881 as the world's first collegiate business school, the Wharton School of the University of Pennsylvania is shaping the future of business by incubating ideas, driving insights, and creating leaders who change the world. With a faculty of more than 235 renowned professors, Wharton has 5,000 undergraduate, MBA, executive MBA, and doctoral students. Each year 18,000 professionals from around the world advance their careers through Wharton Executive Education's individual, company-customized, and online programs. More than 99,000 Wharton alumni form a powerful global network of leaders who transform business every day.

www.wharton.upenn.edu

CPSIA information can be obtained
at www.ICGtesting.com
Printed in the USA
LVHW100639141222
735195LV00002B/289

9 781613 631140